CW00520154

Those Who FORGET

DAG HEWARD-MILLS

Parchment House

First published 2011 by Parchment House
3rd Printing 2014

ISBN : 978-9988-8500-8-1

Find out more about Dag Heward-Mills at:
Healing Jesus Campaign
Write to: evangelist@daghewardmills.org
Website: www.daghewardmills.org
Facebook: Dag Heward-Mills
Twitter: @EvangelistDag

Contents

Chapter 1

The Unrighteousness of Those Who Forget

... God is not unrighteous to forget...
Hebrews 6:10

1. PEOPLE WHO FORGET ARE UNRIGHTEOUS.

FOR GOD *IS* NOT UNRIGHTEOUS TO FORGET your work and labour of love, which ye have shewed toward his name, in that ye have ministered to the saints, and do minister.

Hebrews 6:10

Most people are conscious about the "big four" sins: lying, stealing, fornication and murder. If you were to ask people for a list of sins they are not likely to mention the sin of forgetting. But God's Word is clear on the subject. *Forgetting is unrighteousness!* To forget, to fail to acknowledge, to fail to remember are sins before God.

Can a maid forget her ornaments, or a bride her attire? yet my people have forgotten me days without number.
Jeremiah 2:32

It is incomprehensible to think of some of the things unrighteous people forget.

This classic Scripture on the subject of backsliding shows how a bride will not forget her wedding dress. The wedding dress is the most precious thing to a bride.

Many brides order their wedding dresses long before their weddings. In this Scripture, the absurdity of forgetting God is likened to the unfathomable possibility that a bride would forget her wedding dress.

People grow up and forget who cared for them, who nurtured them and who loved them. They forget those who brought them to Christ, those who raised them in the Lord and those who put them in the ministry. Is it possible that people can forget the people who helped them at the most important crossroads of their lives? Can they turn around and attack the very people who raised them up? The answer is "Yes"! It happens all the time.

People forget God when they prosper. Europe has forsaken God because they have become the richest continent. But it is God who gave them what they have. People become atheists after they become millionaires. What a pathetic sin it is to forget the one who gave you everything! Indeed, it is unrighteousness that is worthy of the most terrible punishment.

2. PEOPLE WHO FORGET ARE UNRIGHTEOUS AND DO NOT HAVE THE NATURE OF GOD.

FOR GOD *IS* NOT UNRIGHTEOUS TO FORGET your work and labour of love, which ye have shewed toward his name, in that ye have ministered to the saints, and do minister.

Hebrews 6:10

God does not forget! Man forgets but God does not forget! People who forget do not have the nature of God! It is the manifestation of the fallen nature of wicked and depraved man to forget things that must never be forgotten.

A person who is controlled by the Word of God and the Spirit of God does not forget certain things.

The natural man does not like to remember those who helped him. The natural unsaved man does not like to remember where he came from. The natural man does not want anyone to know how he came to be who he is.

But that is not the nature of God. When Jesus walked the earth He constantly told us where He came from. He said He could do nothing of Himself.

2

He said He was only speaking the words that His father gave Him.

This is in sharp contrast to the proud man of iniquity. The proud and wicked man does not reveal his origins and beginnings. He believes he is self-made and thinks he came on the scene by his own power.

3. **PEOPLE WHO FORGET ARE UNRIGHTEOUS AND ARE CURSED TO WITHER.**

   Doth the papyrus shoot up without mire? Doth the reed-grass grow without water? Whilst it is yet in his greenness, and not cut down, it WITHERETH before any other herb. So are the paths of ALL THAT FORGET GOD...

   Job 8:11-13

People who forget are cursed to wither. So serious is the sin of forgetting that curses are rained on the lives of forgetful people. You don't need to hear a curse spoken against you for forgetting important things. The Holy Scriptures has already declared that those that forget God shall wither. Be careful that you remember all the ways the Lord has brought you and all the things He has done for you.

4. **UNRIGHTEOUS PEOPLE ARE NOT CONSCIOUS OF THE DANGERS OF FORGETTING.**

   By the rivers of Babylon, there we sat down, yea, we wept, when we remembered Zion.

   We hanged our harps upon the willows in the midst thereof.

   For there they that carried us away captive *required of us* a song; and they that wasted us required of us mirth, *saying,* Sing us *one* of the songs of Zion.

   How shall we sing the LORD'S song in a strange land?

   IF I FORGET THEE, O JERUSALEM, LET MY RIGHT HAND FORGET HER CUNNING.

3

IF I DO NOT REMEMBER THEE, LET MY TONGUE CLEAVE TO THE ROOF OF MY MOUTH; if I prefer not Jerusalem above my chief joy.

Psalms 137:1-6

You must begin to take remembrance very seriously. The psalmist knew that it would be a tragedy to forget Jerusalem. He placed a curse on himself if he did not remember where he came from. This is how serious the issue of remembrance is. You might as well stop living if you do not remember certain things. Your tongue will cleave to the roof of your mouth if you cannot remember where God raised you from. Your right hand will be unable to write cheques when you forget what God has done for you.

5. **UNRIGHTEOUS PEOPLE FORGET GOD WHEN THEY ARE FULL, WHEN THEY HAVE HOUSES AND WHEN THEY ARE RICH.**

LEST WHEN THOU HAST EATEN AND ART FULL, AND HAST BUILT GOODLY HOUSES, and dwelt *therein*; And when thy herds and thy flocks multiply, and thy silver and thy gold is multiplied, and all that thou hast is multiplied; then thine heart be lifted up, and thou forget the Lord thy God, which brought thee forth out of the land of Egypt, from the house of bondage;

Deuteronomy 8:12-14

The unrighteousness of forgetting commonly affects people who are *full*! People who live in their own houses tend to forget God. Those who have multiplied all that they have also quickly forget God. You must become the type of person who is rich and prosperous and yet mindful of where you came from. It is a sad fact that many rich people talk a lot but give little. People speak about the blessings God has given them but they do not honour God for what He has done.

6. UNRIGHTEOUS PEOPLE WHO FORGET ARE OFTEN PROUD.

Lest when thou hast eaten and art full, and hast built goodly houses, and dwelt therein; And when thy herds and thy flocks multiply, and thy silver and thy gold is multiplied, and all that thou hast is multiplied; then THINE HEART BE LIFTED UP, and thou forget the Lord thy God, which brought thee forth out of the land of Egypt, from the house of bondage; And thou say in thine heart, My power and the might of mine hand hath gotten me this wealth.

Deuteronomy 8:12-14, 17

Pride is one of the principal causes of forgetting. People do not want to acknowledge that God helped them.

They don't want to acknowledge that any human being helped them.

They actually think in their hearts that they are self-made and they want you to think same.

These people do not acknowledge God and their hearts are lifted up.

People who do not pay tithes do not acknowledge God's role in their prosperity. When people's hearts are lifted up they say, "I worked hard to get what I have."

The Modern Pagans of Europe

I once asked a rich European woman whether she believed in God. She looked at me in astonishment, almost amazed that I had asked such a "silly" question.

"Of course not," she answered.

Pointing to her chest she said, "I believe in myself. Why should I believe in God?"

I have heard countless Europeans say that Africans believe in God because they don't have solutions to their problems. Modern Europe, which once sent Christianity around the world, is drowned in unbelief and paganism. The hallmark of this demonic blight on Europe is the belief in self and the belief in hard work without God. Europe has fallen into unrighteousness and wickedness because they have forgotten God.

7. UNRIGHTEOUS PEOPLE DO NOT REMEMBER ANYONE WHEN THEY BECOME WEALTHY.

When people become wealthy they very easily forget how they got that wealth. They sort of assume that the wealth came to them through their own efforts but not really through the grace of God.

Have you noticed that there are not many really wealthy people that attend church regularly? Few rich people pay tithes. Most of the tithe payers are salaried workers who do not earn very much.

The business tycoons think they earn "too much to pay tithes". This is why a special warning to remember is given to people that have been given the power to get wealth.

But thou shalt remember the lord thy God: for it is HE THAT GIVETH THEE POWER TO GET WEALTH, that he may establish his covenant which he sware unto thy fathers, as it is this day.

And it shall be, if thou do at all FORGET the LORD thy God, and walk after other gods, and serve them, and worship them, I testify against you this day that ye shall surely perish.

Deuteronomy 8:18-19

8. UNRIGHTEOUS PEOPLE DO NOT REMEMBER THEIR PAST SINS AND MISTAKES.

REMEMBER, and FORGET not, how thou PROVOKEDST THE LORD THY GOD TO WRATH

6

**in the wilderness: from the day that thou didst depart
out of the land of Egypt, until ye came unto this place,
ye have been rebellious against the LORD.**

Deuteronomy 9:7

Why must you remember your sins and mistakes? Because
remembrance of your sins and mistakes makes you recognize
how much grace and mercy has been shown to you.

It also helps you to acknowledge that it is not by any works of
righteousness that you are in His service.

A constant reminder of your past rebelliousness and sinfulness
will keep you in an importantly humble state.

When you forget that you were rebellious you have no
compassion for others who are at the stage you were at some
years ago.

Remembrance of failings is powerful in its ability to induce
humility.

The Broken Pastor

A broken-hearted pastor once said to me, "My wife divorced
me some years ago."

He continued, "Every time I get angry with my staff and begin
to rebuke them, a voice tells me, 'You better shut up because you
couldn't even keep your own wife.'"

I felt so sorry for him.

I had seen this man rebuking and correcting people a few years
earlier. At that time, he seemed to have very little compassion or
understanding for anyone.

But now after being abandoned by his wife he was a completely
different person. As he himself said, every time he remembered
his divorce, he softened his attitude towards other people.

I realized how much more humble he had become after his
divorce.

Remembrance of your past failings is important to keep you on the path of righteousness. When you remember the mistakes you made in the past it will also keep you from going the same way again.

9. UNRIGHTEOUS PEOPLE LIVE IN A LAND OF FORGETFULNESS WHICH IS A PLACE OF DEATH.

Wilt thou shew wonders to the dead? Shall the dead arise and praise thee? Selah.

Shall thy lovingkindness be declared in the grave? Or thy faithfulness in destruction?

Shall thy wonders be known in the dark? AND THY RIGHTEOUSNESS IN THE LAND OF FORGETFULNESS?

Psalms 88:10-12

A minister who dwells in a world of forgetfulness will dwell in a land of death.

The Bible calls the land of forgetfulness the land of death and the grave.

Make sure that you do not dwell in a world where you do not remember important things.

There are ministers who do not remember their spiritual fathers. Such people dwell in the land of forgetfulness, which is a land of death. There are people who do not remember or acknowledge those who helped them. Indeed, you dwell in the midst of death when you forget.

To remember is to give life to your life! To remember is to practise righteousness! God commands us to remember! Remembrance is the will of God!

10. UNRIGHTEOUS PEOPLE FORGET THEIR HUMBLE BEGINNINGS.

And thou shalt REMEMBER THAT THOU WAST A BONDMAN IN THE LAND OF EGYPT, and the Lord

8

thy God redeemed thee: therefore I command thee this thing to day.

Deuteronomy 15:15

The unrighteous man will forget that he was once a bondman. Remembering your humble beginnings is crucial in your fight against pride. Most great people have humble beginnings. Most great people have difficulties that they have risen out of. If people on earth were to remember where they came from, there would be a million times more love, understanding and compassion in the world. Indeed, there would be nicer bosses and kinder leaders everywhere.

11. UNRIGHTEOUS PEOPLE FORGET AFTER A SHORT WHILE.

Only take heed to thyself, and keep thy soul diligently, lest thou forget the things which thine eyes have seen, and LEST THEY DEPART FROM THY HEART ALL THE DAYS OF THY LIFE: but teach them thy sons, and thy sons' sons;

Deuteronomy 4:9

Some things must never depart from your heart all the days of your life. It is important to remember some things for the rest of your life. When the Lord has done great things for you, you are not expected to remember it for only five years. Many people do not realize that they are indebted to God forever. It is not about remembering for a number of years. It is about remembering for the rest of your life. People remember their salvation for a few years and "mature" to a place where they never talk about salvation. How sad that is!

A young rebellious pastor once said about his spiritual father, "I don't owe him anything. I've honoured him enough." But he was making a mistake. He did owe him gratitude and honour for the rest of his life because what had been done for him had affected his *whole life*. Paul told Philemon, "You owe me your whole life."

Another puffed up pastor said to me, "I've served you for five years. I don't owe you anything." In effect, he was asking, "Do you want me to be grateful forever?" The answer is, "Yes, you must be grateful forever."

12. UNRIGHTEOUS PEOPLE FORGET THEIR COVENANTS AND AGREEMENTS.

Everyone will make a number of covenants in his life. For example, you may make a covenant to follow Christ, a covenant of obedience or a covenant of marriage. Often, by the time one side of the agreement is fulfilled people forget to fulfil their obligations. That is why covenants are made.

As sin has increased in the world the ability to remember has also decreased. As time has gone by, the word of mouth has virtually lost its value and come to be replaced by written documents. Sinful man has become a covenant breaker (Romans 1:31).

Take heed unto yourselves, LEST YE FORGET THE COVENANT OF THE LORD your God, which he made with you, and make you a graven image, or the likeness of any thing, which the LORD thy God hath forbidden thee.

Deuteronomy 4:23

13. BECAUSE UNRIGHTEOUS PEOPLE FORGET GOD, GOD WILL FORGET THEIR CHILDREN.

My people are destroyed for lack of knowledge: because thou hast rejected knowledge, I will also reject thee, that thou shalt be no priest to me: SEEING THOU HAST FORGOTTEN THE LAW OF THY GOD, I WILL ALSO FORGET THY CHILDREN.

Hosea 4:6

There are many curses that follow people who forget God. What will happen if God forgets your children? They will be given over to the devil. Their hearts will not be touched to love

God. They will become vagabonds, uprooted trees and wandering stars. They will be exposed to the wicked devices of Satan.

No parent is capable of totally controlling his children. It takes the grace of God. If God forgets your children there is no hope for them. Do not forget so that He will not forget your children!

14. BECAUSE UNRIGHTEOUS PEOPLE FORGET GOD, GOD WILL SEND FIRE INTO THEIR LIVES.

FOR ISRAEL HATH FORGOTTEN HIS MAKER, and buildeth temples; and Judah hath multiplied fenced cities: BUT I WILL SEND A FIRE UPON HIS CITIES, and it shall devour the palaces thereof.

Hosea 8:14

Another curse that follows people who forget is fire! Fire speaks of trouble, destruction and damnation. Perhaps you have not considered how dangerous the sin of forgetfulness is. Forgetfulness attracts many a curse. May your life be delivered from the fire that devours men who lack remembrance!

15. BECAUSE UNRIGHTEOUS PEOPLE FORGET GOD THEY WILL BE SENT TO HELL.

The wicked shall be turned into hell, and all the nations that forget God.

Psalm 9:17

People who forget God will be turned into Hell. Hell is a large lake of fire waiting to burn men who do not want to remember the most important person in this life – their maker.

The Scriptures are clear. God will throw out the people who have forgotten His name. You do not want to go to Hell. But Hell is reserved for those who forget God. Forgetting God is the ultimate unrighteousness of man.

Forgetting God is a more serious crime than we have wanted to believe.

Chapter 2

Six Reasons Why It Is Important to Remember

And THOU SHALT REMEMBER that thou wast a bondman in Egypt: and thou shalt observe and do these statutes.

Deuteronomy 16:12

Amongst the people you will work with are men who do not have the ability to REMEMBER. Men without remembrance are a most deadly group. They are the brewing conspirators of your ministry. They are the up and coming traitors of your team.

The ability to remember is probably the single most important quality for a minister. I am set at ease when I discover that I am relating with someone who has the ability to remember. Almost every disloyal person lacks the ability to remember! When I think of some of the strange sons that I have had, I wonder if they cannot remember the times I had with them.

When the children of Israel were coming out of Egypt, remembrance was one thing God wanted them to have. He wanted them to remember how He had brought them out of Egypt. He wanted them to remember how bad things had been there. In their prosperity, He wanted them to remember the Lord God. God knew what would happen if they forgot these important things.

1. **Remembrance makes you appreciate salvation and preach about salvation.**

Men without remembrance sing songs that show their short memory. Most Christians are not grateful to God for their salvation.

Sadly, many Christians do not remember what Christ has done for them. The songs composed and sang by Christians today reflect this forgetful and unfaithful attitude. My heart jumps when I hear songs about salvation. Perhaps, this is why I love songs that speak of our salvation.

Men without remembrance do not evangelize. They have forgotten how salvation came to them. They have even forgotten how salvation gets to anyone.

Pastors who have forgotten about their salvation preach without doing altar calls. Men without remembrance have substituted the message of salvation for the popular motivational sermons on finance, management and "prosperity". These messages may be good but they cannot be substituted for the message of salvation.

It is Christians without remembrance who go round the world giving out food and water to sinners without ever preaching to them. Perhaps they have forgotten that no one will go to Heaven unless he is born again.

Churches are filled with happy-go-lucky Christians who want to celebrate their prosperity without a thought about how they got saved. What about others? Would I have been saved if no one had remembered?

2.   Remembrance makes you walk in your calling.

And THOU SHALT REMEMBER that thou wast a bondman in the land of Egypt, and the LORD thy God redeemed thee: therefore I command thee this thing to day.

Deuteronomy 15:15

I remember that I got saved in secondary school. I was about fifteen years old when I found the Lord. The memory of how I found Christ stays with me. I feel so blessed and favoured to be chosen and saved. The memory of it guides me in my current ministry. I find myself preaching in schools and universities. I have great hope when I see young boys and girls walking forward to receive Jesus Christ. I remember that I too gave my heart to the Lord in school. Some people seem to remember nothing. Perhaps salvation means nothing to them.

Some men who were raised in orphanages remember how they were shown the love of God. Some of them have built orphanages and cared for other children because they remember everything. Others walk away and rewrite their history, deleting every memory of the orphanage.

The Memory of the Missionaries

The memory of what God has brought you through is supposed to guide your present-day ministry. When I see the cemeteries of white missionaries, I remember how they shed their blood on Ghanaian soil for the salvation of an entire nation. Then I think of other remote nations, which are waiting for similar missionaries to come.

"Will anyone go?" I ask myself. "Will an entire nation perish because there is no missionary?"

I remember the sacrifice of these Swiss missionaries with gratitude. It is because Ghanaian churches are led by pastors who have *forgotten* about how missionaries came to die in Ghana, that they do not send missionaries to other similarly deprived areas.

3. Remembrance keeps you humble.

When you remember where you came from, you always recognize that the grace of God has been at work. When you clearly remember where God picked you up from, you will not attribute your current success to any personal strengths or wisdom. Unfortunately, people tend to black out their past. They refer to no one and they seem to remember nothing bad or difficult from their background.

Listening to them, you get the impression that they are self-made. They do not mention their beginnings, their struggles or their failings. You almost get the impression that you are reading about superman when you read about them!

But Paul said that he took pleasure in his infirmities and distressing situations. Paul told us that he had been beaten and whipped by unbelievers. This does not sound like superman.

Talking plainly about things God has brought you through will only make you thankful and humble. It will save you from self-deception and unnecessary pride.

... Most gladly, therefore, I will rather boast about my weaknesses, so that the power of Christ may dwell in me.

2 Corinthians 12:9, NASB

A man of remembrance stays humble through the memories of his different trials and sufferings. It is wiser to share these difficulties than to share your victories. I have noticed how the Lord has helped me to share my uselessness with others.

Sometimes I end my sermons on a note of weakness and defeat. I take pleasure in the weakness that is real so that the power of Christ will rest on me.

I have seen the dead raised in my ministry but I have also seen many people die after I prayed for them. There are times I think about the powerlessness and uselessness of my life and ministry. I am learning to choose this way so that the power of Christ will rest on me.

There is no need to protect an image that needs no protection. Be real! Remember the realities of your life. Share them and help yourself to be humble.

4. Remembrance makes you a grateful person.

The sin of ungratefulness is as the sin of forgetfulness. They are almost synonymous. Sadly, people forget how they have been loved. Because people forget exactly how they were helped, they are indifferent to the source of help.

Some parents virtually have to beg their children to remember them in their old age. Some pastors virtually have to beg their congregations to honour them for their labours.

This world has six billion, ungrateful and forgetful people! This is what creates the discontentment, conflict and wars. There are people we must be grateful to. God wants us to be thankful and grateful for all His blessings. We must be grateful for the channels that God uses. We must be grateful for their faithfulness with what God gave to them.

5. Remembrance makes you kind and helpful to others.

Remembrance is important because it is supposed to govern your current behaviour.

> **And thou shalt REMEMBER that thou wast a bondman in Egypt: and thou shalt observe and do these statutes.**
> **Deuteronomy 16:12**

The Israelites were supposed to remember their past and allow this memory to influence their current behaviour.

In the Scripture I just quoted, remembering their past state of being bondmen would propel them to obey the Lord and include the fatherless, widows and strangers in their feasts of rejoicing.

> **And thou shalt rejoice before the LORD thy God, thou, and thy son, and thy daughter, and thy manservant, and thy maidservant, and the Levite that is within thy gates, and the stranger, and the fatherless, and the widow, that are among you, in the place which the LORD thy God hath chosen to place his name there.**
> **And thou shalt REMEMBER that thou wast a bondman in Egypt: and thou shalt observe and do these statutes.**
> **Deuteronomy 16:11-12**

You Can't Stay Here

When you do not remember where you came from, you behave wrongly. One day, I noticed a lady who was constantly irritated by a stream of cousins, nieces and nephews who were living with her.

She did not want to have all these relations living in her house. She wanted her privacy. She wanted to enjoy her husband, her home and her children without interruption. But her husband insisted on having all these cousins, nieces, nephews and miscellaneous relations in the house.

The conflict that this situation was brewing brought the problem to my attention.

One day I asked my wife, "What type of home did this lady grow up in? Did she live with her Daddy, her Mummy and other brothers and sisters?" (You see, my wife knows everything).

My wife smiled and answered, "No, not at all, she didn't."
"So what kind of home did she grow up in?" I asked.
"Oh, she lived with her aunty for most of her early days. Her mother had travelled away for most of her childhood and she grew up living in other people's homes."

Then I thought to myself, "Has this lady forgotten that she was a guest and maybe a bother to someone for many years? Can she not accommodate relatives as she was once accommodated?" The problem is that people forget where they came from.

I remember that it was not easy to break out in ministry. I felt so intimidated by senior "big shot" ministers. They commanded crowds and crowds of people and seemed so powerful.

"How would my ministry ever be like this?" I wondered.

I Was Mocked

One afternoon, I met the pastor of a large church at a social function. He looked me up and down and said, "Pastor Dag." When he addressed me as "Pastor", I felt silly and withered under his mocking smile. You see, I had about twenty people in my church and he had thousands! I felt like an idiot. His voice reeked of contempt. I almost blurted out, "Are you mocking me?" I felt no help from this great man of God - only mockery.

When I began my church, I made several efforts to be accepted and to gain help. I went to see the pastor of a large church in my city. I had to travel to the upscale part of the city to see this pastor. He graciously received me and sat with me in his garden. I told him how I had begun a church. When he began to talk, however, I wished I had never gone there.

I Was Rejected

He said, "There are many young boys who are starting churches without attending Bible schools. They do not know what they are doing. They will all amount to nothing." Every time I read the comment that Nabal made about David, I remember that day because the remarks Nabal made about David were very similar to what this man of God said to me.

And Nabal answered David's servants, and said, Who is David? and who is the son of Jesse? there be many servants now a days that break away every man from his master.

1 Samuel 25:10

Instead of helping me, he sent his associate pastor to organize a large crusade right where I had started the church. During the programme, they showed a documentary of this pastor's ministry and I felt foolish for even trying to begin a church. But I did not give up. I was still looking for recognition and help for my fledgling church. I invited another well-known pastor to minister in my baby church. This fellow had ministered in my fellowship many times.

Who Are the Thorns?

This time he told my assistant who was sent to invite him that he would not come. "Why not?" I asked.

My pastor was hesitant to answer my question. Finally, he did. He said, "The *big minister* said, 'I have stopped sowing amongst thorns'."

"Thorns?" I asked. "Who are the thorns? When did we become thorns? He doesn't want to preach to us anymore?" I questioned.

"Yes," the messenger answered. "He will not come to this new church and he has given the reason. He does not sow among thorns anymore."

Nobody helped us when we were small. And I remember each encounter. That is why I try to help others in ministry. I love to encourage up and coming ministers and to tell them that they are going to make it. Nobody ever told me that. Even up till now, nobody tells me that I am going to make it. It is a great thing to be encouraged.

6.   Remembrance makes you kind.

God told the Israelites to be kind to strangers just because they were once foreigners in Egypt.

You shall not oppress a stranger, since you yourselves know the feelings of a stranger, for you also were strangers in the land of Egypt.

Exodus 23:9, NASB

I remember how I suffered under the repression of some lecturers in medical school. Many lecturers had only threats and warnings for their students.

I thought to myself, "If I was ever a lecturer I would be kind to the students and help them to pass their exams."

One day, however, I was chatting with one of my classmates and he said, "When I become a lecturer I will ensure that students suffer as much as I did."

I was amazed at his declaration. Could he not see what he was going through? Would he not remember the anguish that he experienced in this place?

Unfortunately, wicked people do not remember their hardships. Many wicked people simply cannot remember what it was like to be on the other side. God warns us in His Word to remember how we felt and to help others who are in a similar situation.

Perhaps you come from a very poor background. God expects you to reach out and help such poor people because you know what it feels like to be poor!

Chapter 3

Five Evils That Befall
People Who Forget

1. PEOPLE WHO FORGET ARE CONSTANTLY DEMOTED.

Pride goeth before destruction, and an haughty spirit before a fall.

Proverbs 16:18

People fail exams because they do not remember important things. Can you remember when you did your geography examinations and were asked: What is the longest river in the world? What is the highest mountain in the world? What is the largest lake in the world?

I Want to Be Promoted but I Cannot Remember My Geography

But you could not remember the answers to any of these questions. You said that the longest river in the world was the River Jordan. You said that the highest mountain in the world was the Mount of Olives. You said that the largest lake in the world was the Sea of Galilee.

How could you pass your geography examinations when you could not remember that the longest river in the world is the Nile, and the highest mountain is Mount Everest and the largest lake in the world is the Caspian Sea?

Because you could not remember any of these things you could not pass your exams. And because you could not pass your exams, you could not be promoted. Everyone else went ahead whilst you stayed behind.

I Want to Be a Doctor But I Cannot Remember
My Biology

Then you wanted to become a doctor! But how could you become a doctor when you could not remember the answers to simple biology questions? You were asked: " Where is meat digested?" And you answered, "Meat is digested in the rectum." You could not remember that meat is digested in the stomach.

Then you were asked, "Give some examples of carbohydrates?" And you answered, "Fried Fish and pork chops." You could not remember the difference between carbohydrates and protein. Then you were asked, "Where can digestive enzymes be found?" And you answered, "Digestive enzymes are found in the fallopian tubes." With such answers you cannot expect to pass your biology exams. Your inability to remember important biological facts cost you your career in medicine.

Because of this, you could not be chosen for the science class and you never became a doctor.

Simply because you could not remember, you were excluded from the people who went ahead to become medical doctors. Today, you are in a lower social stratum because you could not remember your biology answers.

How Forgetting Leads to Demotion

This same principle applies in spiritual things. Because you cannot remember the Word of God, you keep lowering yourself. Because you cannot remember those who helped you, you keep falling into the group of forgetful and accursed sons. You keep going lower in the ministry because you can't remember the things a minister must never forget.

Most people cannot trace the calamities of their life to their inability to remember. They often blame other things as the causes of their problems. But actually, many of the evils that befall Christians come about only because they fail to remember certain things. Indeed, few people attribute the evils that befall them to forgetting. This is how it happens:

21

Forgetting leads to grumbling, murmuring, discontentment, pride and a host of other evils. When these evils are established, they in turn lead to your destruction and demotion. Are murmuring, discontentment, bitterness and pride not the forerunners of destruction and demotion?

2. FORGETFUL PEOPLE BECOME MURMURERS.

How oft did they provoke him in the wilderness, and grieve him in the desert!

Yea, they turned back and tempted God, and limited the Holy One of Israel.

They REMEMBERED NOT his hand, nor the day when he delivered them from the enemy.

Psalms 78:40-42

The children of Israel are the starkest example of ungrateful and forgetful people. This example is there because we are all like that. We need deliverance from the sin of forgetfulness. Do not think that anything in the Bible is far-fetched and does not apply to you. That is the best way to make the Bible impractical and irrelevant.

If you are a pastor, see all the kings in the Bible as pastors and put yourself in their shoes. See yourself as capable of making all their mistakes. This will help you to learn about yourself.

The children of Israel murmured against God continually. Yet, they had been delivered from being slaves. They had been delivered from being second-rate citizens in the land of Egypt. They had been delivered from the whips of the Egyptian taskmasters. All this did not seem to register in their minds. Have the things that God has done in your life registered on your mind and heart?

After this the Lord took them through the Red Sea. Who had ever walked through the sea? Who has ever walked through the sea since then? He gave them a pillar of fire by night and a pillar of cloud by day. Yet all these did not register on the hearts of the Israelites. They turned against Moses at every opportunity.

They murmured against the Most High and provoked Him to the uttermost.

With this forgetful attitude the children of Israel generated a frenzied crowd of fearful people. Panic whipped through the congregation and no one believed in Moses any longer. Forgetting the great things God had done, led to the historic failure of God's people to enter the Promised Land.

The children of Israel complained about many different things. Nothing seemed to satisfy them. They turned against God who had blessed them and given them many precious things.

Because murmuring emanates from an evil spirit, there is a point at which it does not even make sense. It is a repeated act of rebellion against a person. It is anointed from Hell and fully controlled by an evil being. Avoid people who murmur like you are avoiding the plague!

Notice the complaints of the children of Israel. Their complaints, if analyzed, look almost like the senseless gibberish of crazed monkeys.

"We remember the fish, which we did eat in Egypt freely; the cucumbers, and the melons, and the leeks, and the onions, and the garlick: But our soul is dried away: there is nothing at all, beside this manna, before our eyes" (Numbers 11:5-6).

What else would a slave desire more than freedom from slavery? And yet this benefit seemed not to register on their minds. They seemed to suffer from amnesia of a sort.

Notice how irrational and ridiculous these grumblings were: they complained about not having garlic, onions and leeks! Don't you think any present-day prisoner would prefer to be set free from prison than to have a daily supply of garlic?

Every prisoner in the world would gladly accept freedom if they never eat garlic again! Please do not let forgetfulness lead you to madness!

3. PEOPLE WHO FORGET ARE REJECTED.

Forgetting led to murmuring and murmuring led to God's rejection. God will reject you when you complain. It is important to be thankful all the time. Giving thanks is one of the things that help you to be filled with the Holy Spirit.

... BE FILLED WITH THE SPIRIT; Speaking to yourselves in psalms and hymns and spiritual songs, singing and making melody in your heart to the Lord; GIVING THANKS always for all things unto God and the Father in the name of our Lord Jesus Christ,

Ephesians 5:18-20

Just as giving thanks makes you filled with the Holy Spirit, complaining and murmuring will cause you to be filled with demons. The children of Israel were possessed with devils as they complained against Almighty God. The spirit of death killed them in the wilderness. If the Israelites had remembered all the great things the Lord had done, they would have stayed in the grace of God.

Jesus taught this principle to His disciples. He wanted them to remember what had happened in the past. He wanted them to remember previous miracles and breakthroughs. He wanted them to remember the whole picture.

When He spoke of the leaven of the Pharisees, the disciples thought He meant real bread. They did not remember the miracle of the five thousand loaves. If they had remembered this miracle, they would not have thought that his comment was referring to real bread.

And the disciples came to the other side of the sea, but they had forgotten to bring any bread.

And Jesus said to them, "Watch out and beware of the leaven of the Pharisees and Sadducees."

They began to discuss this among themselves, saying, "He said that because we did not bring any bread."

But Jesus, aware of this, said, "You men of little faith, why do you discuss among yourselves that you have no bread?

Do you not yet understand or REMEMBER the five loaves of the five thousand, and how many baskets full you picked up? Or the seven loaves of the four thousand, and how many large baskets full you picked up?"

Matthew 16:5-10, NASB

He Forgot

Without realizing it, I have often rejected people who complained and murmured about their work. I prefer to keep an employee who is incompetent but has a good attitude. As soon as people complain, they become unattractive. It is actually repulsive to have a complaining and discontented person around you.

I remember a brother who rebelled against me and said many unpleasant things. He became a most repulsive individual to me. As I heard of the various things that he said about me, I could only liken him to a bad dream! He used to love me and look up to me but, he had turned around a hundred and eighty degrees and now called me the devil. He hurled insults against those who led him to Christ.

He felt he was not being treated fairly and complained about his conditions of service. He spoke about how little money he was earning, and complained that he would have been earning millions if he had stayed in his former job. Doesn't that sound familiar? Doesn't it sound like the children of Israel claiming they would have been better off in Egypt?

And the children of Israel said unto them, Would to God we had died by the hand of the LORD in the land of Egypt, when we sat by the flesh pots, and when we did eat bread to the full; for ye have brought us forth

into this wilderness, to kill this whole assembly with hunger.

Exodus 16:3

This fellow had forgotten how I had welcomed him into full-time ministry.

He had forgotten how he had said, "I will work for God, even if I am not paid."

He had forgotten the times of fellowship we enjoyed together and how we were like brothers from the same family.

He had forgotten how he loved listening to my tapes.

He had forgotten how he would lie down for hours soaking in messages from different camp meetings I had preached at.

It seemed he had forgotten how I had appointed him as a pastor.

He probably could not remember how I ordained him into the ministry.

He had forgotten how he had never been able to travel outside the country until I arranged for his first visa.

I do not think that I am harming someone when he comes to work in full-time ministry. I believe that full-time ministry is the greatest opportunity of a lifetime. If, however, the person feels it is a punishment, I would not like to continue inflicting hardships on the person.

After this fellow began his complaints and grumblings, our relationship was at the beginning of the end! It was only a matter of time before he was incompatible with what God was doing in my ministry. When the children of Israel began to complain against Moses, they became incompatible with the Promised Land vision. When you complain you will be rejected. This is what happened to God's people as they marched to the Promised Land. Only little children who did not understand and who could not complain entered the Promised Land.

The Discontented Missionaries

Some years ago, some missionaries I had sent to the mission field began complaining about various things. They would call one another and gossip about how they were not being treated fairly. Through no fault of the Missions Office, one of them was separated from his wife and felt that his wife's trip to join him was being unduly delayed.

Another missionary complained about the routing of his wife's flight. Other missionaries joined in and became equally discontented about other issues. Different little issues became mountains of fodder for discussion.

After a while, the spirit of discontentment, murmuring and grumbling was rife amongst this team of missionaries.

I remember a meeting I had with them. They all seemed different from the people I had known. I wondered how they had become so forgetful so soon.

These young men had forgotten how I had helped them to come into ministry.

They had forgotten how I had flown them into international cities and set them up to start churches.

They had forgotten that they had never had to rent a house since they finished school.

They had forgotten that their daily bread was guaranteed, whether the church they pastored made enough money or not.

They had forgotten that cars were handed over to them on a silver platter.

They never needed to know the price of a car.

They had forgotten the times of fellowship and love I had had with them.

They had forgotten how I had visited them in their homes and become close to them.

They had forgotten my involvement in their personal lives.

They had forgotten how I would sit, chat and fellowship with them.

They had forgotten how I had helped them to choose marriage partners.

They had forgotten how I had encouraged and guided them in the ministry when they were in university.

They had forgotten how I helped them to have their weddings.

They had forgotten how I sent them on honeymoons and paid for everything.

They had forgotten that they did not need to know the price of a plane ticket - it was just bought for them.

They had forgotten how privileged they were to have been sent to countries they had never known.

As I sat at the meeting, I realized that my young missionaries had forgotten too many things too soon. They had become grumpy, disgruntled and discontented with the ministry and with me. It was as though another spirit had taken over their lives.

I held on for as long as I could but I had to dismiss them from the mission field and from full-time ministry.

It was a painful and very difficult decision but there was no way out. I had no choice but to take the decision to dismiss them. These were beloved sons of mine and I knew that what I was doing would change their lives drastically. These soldiers would not be a part of what I was doing and I would march on without them.

Forgetting had cost them too much. May you not forget what the Lord has done in your life!

4.   PEOPLE WHO FORGET BECOME DISLOYAL.

> ... Judas Iscariot, which also betrayed him...
>
> **Mark 3:19**

Judas was the all-time traitor of traitors. How did he become the most treacherous and disloyal follower of all time? The answer may lie in this important subject of remembrance. Forgetting important things makes you fail school exams as well as all the other tests of life.

Perhaps, Judas forgot many of the miracles that Jesus did.

He forgot how he was chosen from among hundreds of awestruck followers.

He forgot how he was privileged to sit with the Lord in private and to fellowship with deity.

He forgot how he had heard many things that no one had ever heard.

He forgot how he had listened to teachings that had never ever been recorded.

He forgot the breakfasts and lunches he had had with the Lord.

He forgot how he was chosen from among the twelve to handle money.

He forgot how Jesus had trusted him especially with a unique job He had given to no one else.

It seemed he had forgotten about the mansions promised in Heaven.

The fact that he was to have rewards in Heaven meant nothing to him.

Judas forgot about the frightening messages of Heaven and Hell.

Judas forgot about the rich man and Lazarus (people they actually knew and remembered) and how Jesus had told them that they were in Hell and Heaven.

Judas had forgotten the powerful messages that Jesus had preached.

Judas had forgotten about the amazing miracles Jesus had performed when he healed blind, deaf and dumb people.

You see, if you remember certain things they will restrain you when you are going the wrong way. If Judas had remembered the supernatural nature of Christ, he would have been hesitant to betray God. Judas did not remember how Jesus had raised people from the dead.

Perhaps if he had remembered how Jesus had raised Lazarus from the dead after four days, he would have dropped the whole idea of betraying the Son of God.

29

Perhaps a chill would have gone down his spine when he remembered that Jesus had actually predicted that he would die and rise again after three days.

Sadly, Judas' mind was fixated on the thirty pieces of silver he had been promised. Somehow, this fixation blacked out the memory of how supernatural and powerful Jesus really was.

What is your mind fixated on? Which memories have you blacked out? Have you forgotten something important? Could this lack of remembrance lead to your annihilation? Will you become like Judas and forget all that has happened? Can it be that you will forget all your experiences and not remember anything that was said?

What did Jesus say about Judas? He said, "It would be better if he had never been born." He did not say this about anyone, including the murderers and thieves He encountered. He said to the thief on the cross, "Today you will be with me in paradise." But He said about Judas, "It would have been better that you were not born!" Mercies!!

5. PEOPLE WHO FORGET REPEAT MISTAKES

The Bible story of Belshazzar is an example of how a son repeats the sins of his father because he forgets. God does not tell us the stories of our fathers in order to disgrace or discredit them. Actually, none of us would like the stories of our low moments to be repeated publicly. However, God has allowed the mistakes of His servants to be written for our admonishing that we may not repeat them.

Unfortunately, history shows that people simply repeat the same mistakes over and over again. Will we stay away from the sins that He warns us about through our fathers?

When Daniel rebuked King Belshazzar (son of Nebuchadnezzar), he told him that he had not learnt humility even though his father had fallen through pride.

Then Daniel answered and said before the king, Let thy gifts be to thyself, and give thy rewards to another; yet

I will read the writing unto the king, and make known
to him the interpretation.

O thou king, the most high God gave Nebuchadnezzar
thy father a kingdom, and majesty, and glory, and
honour:

And for the majesty that he gave him, all people,
nations, and languages, trembled and feared before
him: whom he would he slew; and whom he would he
kept alive; and whom he would he set up; and whom he
would he put down.

But when his heart was lifted up, and his mind hardened
in pride, he was deposed from his kingly throne, and
they took his glory from him:

And he was driven from the sons of men; and his heart
was made like the beasts, and his dwelling was with the
wild asses: they fed him with grass like oxen, and his
body was wet with the dew of heaven; till he knew that
the most high God ruled in the kingdom of men, and
that he appointeth over it whomsoever he will.

AND THOU HIS SON, O BELSHAZZAR, HAST
NOT HUMBLED THINE HEART, THOUGH THOU
KNEWEST ALL THIS;

But hast lifted up thyself against the LORD of heaven...

Daniel 5:17-23

The Pastors' Meeting

One day, I had a meeting with some pastors on the third floor
of our church building. We discussed several issues that related to
loyalty and church government. There were many contributions
to the discussion and the pastors felt free to share what they felt.

At a point, we discussed a particular situation in which
a pastor had taken over and renamed a branch church. We
discussed and condemned how he had painted over the old name
and replaced it with a new name. Everyone agreed that this was
unacceptable behaviour. A particular pastor stood up and gave

a speech. He condemned such treacherous acts and pledged his unflinching support for the ministry. He virtually promised to give up anything that would hinder his lifelong commitment.

A few months later, this same speech-giving brother came up to me and said, "I have decided to start a church." I was taken aback because he was already pastoring a church.

So I asked, "Which church are you going to start? I thought you were already pastoring a church."

Then he said, "God has led me to start a church."

I continued, "Is it a Lighthouse church or another church."

He answered, "Another church."

I asked him, "What happens to the Lighthouse church you are pastoring?" But he did not answer.

The answer came several days later when he painted over the name, "Lighthouse Chapel International" and replaced it with a new name. It was surprising because this very pastor had shown such strong and vocal support for the ministry at the meeting. He had been part of the discussion that condemned the "stealing" of churches. Just like Belshazzar, he repeated exactly what someone ahead of him had done.

Let us all pray that God's grace will keep us from repeating the sins and mistakes of our fathers. God allows us to know the mistakes of seniors so that we stay away from them. We are not better than people ahead of us. Neither do we have any better motives nor prayer lives than anyone ahead of us. It is the grace of God that will keep us from evil. Pray that your Daddy's devil will not be your devil!

Chapter 4

Eight Common Mistakes
of People Who Forget

1. PEOPLE WHO FORGET DISHONOUR FOUNDERS AND FATHERS.

And Ham, the father of Canaan, saw the nakedness of his father, and told his two brethren without.

Genesis 9:22

One of the commonest occurrences is the forgetting of the contribution of fathers and founders. Our Lord Jesus knew that He would be forgotten by the church, so He instituted the ritual of Holy Communion so that we would remember Him.

Recently, I was preaching to the leaders of student churches at the university. I called for the leader of a particular church. The leader stepped forward and I asked, "Do you know that I started the church you are pastoring?"

This pastor looked surprised and answered, "No, I never knew."

So I informed him about how I spent two and a half years of my university life praying, fasting and preaching till his church was established.

This Christian leader had no idea how I had been maligned and criticized for establishing his church. But such is the lot of fathers and founders. Their contribution is often forgotten. Unfortunately, in so doing, many set aside the ideals and vision the founders had.

One day, a brother who had set up a mass choir returned to his university campus to pay a visit. He was greeted at the door by an usher who, obviously, did not know that he was talking to one

33

of the founders of what he was enjoying and managing. He was treated as a common stranger and ushered unceremoniously to the very back of the hall. Such is the lot of the founder!

Many churches do not remember their founders. The memory of the founder dims as the years go by. His name is pushed away and anything that reminds them of him is erased. New pastors want to remove the concept of the "Founder's Day". The new pastor wants the picture of the founder taken away.

The current pastor loves to be seen as the luminary who achieved everything on his own. Such people have forgotten the work that the founder did for the church to come into existence.

The work of a founder and the apostle is the most difficult job of all.

Paul said of founders:

... I think that God hath set forth us the apostles last, as it were appointed to death: for we are made a spectacle unto the world, and to angels, and to men
1 Corinthians 4:9

The founder's work is buried in the ground and many do not see it. Many founders are scarred and wounded individuals. They receive the largest amount of criticism and the least amount of appreciation.

The families of apostles and founders are not exempted from this treatment. They are often set aside and forgotten. The family may have paid an equally high price for the founder to lay the foundation he did.

Upon the death of founders and apostles, many are moved with compassion for their families and declare that they will set up foundations and trust funds for them.

Sadly, with the passage of time, the passion for setting up these foundations and mobilizing the money that is needed fades away. The family of the founder is left to fend for itself and to fight for survival.

The Forgotten Founder

I remember one founder who died and left behind little children and a pregnant wife. He also left behind a thriving ministry with many large churches.

Years after the death of her husband, she was without sustenance and help from the church he had founded.

In desperation, his wife remarried.

One day, I asked, "Who did the founder's wife eventually get married to?"

I must admit that I was stunned by the answer. I was told that this great founder's wife had married one of her husband's servants.

I thought to myself, "She must have been desperate."

I remembered one of the churches of this great founder that I had preached in. It was large and prosperous. I wondered if these large churches could not take care of this widow. Such is the lot of founders - so easily forgotten and so easily dismissed from memory.

The Forgotten Ideals

Perhaps it is even more painful when the founder's ideals are set aside. I once read about a great founder and found no comparison between what he believed in and what the church he had founded was practising.

I visited the grave of this great founder and was taken on a tour of the founder's home by the caretaker. One of the last comments the caretaker made was indeed very sad.

He said, "This great founder would be very sad if he rose from the dead today."

"Why?" I asked.

He continued, "Most of the vices he fought against are the ones that currently plague the church he founded."

Sadly, the founder's ideals had been set aside. Even though this founder's name is certainly not forgotten, his ideals and vision have been set aside.

The danger of all this is that the curse of dishonouring fathers will follow the current leaders.

Ham Forgot

It is an important principle to honour fathers. Ham, the black son of Noah, broke this principle and dishonoured his father. It is the curse that followed that governs large sections of the world's population.

Across the world, the inability of the black man to rise above the state of servanthood can only be explained by a curse. Others may differ in their view and I can handle that, but I find it difficult to explain the state of Africa and black people, in general, except by interpreting it as the curse of Ham. This severe curse came about when a young man forgot the contribution his father had made to his existence.

And Ham, the father of Canaan, saw the nakedness of his father, and told his two brethren without.
Genesis 9:22

Ham forgot that it was his father, Noah, who heard from God and obeyed the call.

Ham forgot that he did not know God well enough to hear the voice that commanded to build an ark.

Ham forgot that if his father had not built the ark he would have drowned along with the rest of the world.

By faith Noah, being warned of God of things not seen as yet, moved with fear, prepared an ark to the saving

of his house; by the which he condemned the world, and became heir of the righteousness which is by faith.
Hebrews 11:7

Ham forgot that God had judged Noah to be a righteous man. "But Noah found grace in the eyes of the Lord" (Genesis 6:8). Ham forgot that he was alive only because of his "drunken" father whom God found righteous.

Ham forgot that every man of God has a right to be naked in his own tent.

Ham forgot that he himself was, sometimes, naked in his own tent. He forgot too many things and he paid dearly for his lack of remembrance.

Today, the black man can scarcely rise out of the waters of worldwide despisement.

2. PEOPLE WHO FORGET BECOME DISOBEDIENT.

Jeroboam was chosen by the Lord to replace Solomon. Jeroboam, a "nobody", was picked to replace the ruling lineage of David and Solomon; the two greatest kings of Israel. This honour was done to Jeroboam because Solomon had gone after idols and worshipped false gods.

And Ahijah caught the new garment that was on him, and rent it in twelve pieces:

And he said to JEROBOAM, Take thee ten pieces: for thus saith the Lord, the God of Israel, Behold, I will rend the kingdom out of the hand of Solomon, and will give ten tribes to thee:

(But he shall have one tribe for my servant David's sake, and for Jerusalem's sake, the city which I have chosen out of all the tribes of Israel:)

Because that they have forsaken me, and have worshipped Ashtoreth the goddess of the Zidonians, Chemosh the god of the Moabites, and Milcom the god of the children of Ammon, and have not walked in my

ways, to do that which is right in mine eyes, and to keep
my statutes and my judgments, as did David his father.

1 Kings 11:30-33

Somehow, when Jeroboam became the king, he forgot why he
was chosen in the first place. He forgot why God had chosen him
as the replacement of the lineage of David and Solomon.

He forgot the most important thing and disobeyed the Lord in
exactly the same way Solomon had. Notice the passages, which
reveal both the privileged calling of Jeroboam and the subsequent
repetition by Jeroboam of Solomon's sins.

**And JEROBOAM said in his heart, now shall the
kingdom return to the house of David:**

**If this people go up to do sacrifice in the house of the
Lord at Jerusalem, then shall the heart of this people
turn again unto their lord, even unto Rehoboam
king of Judah, and they shall kill me, and go again to
Rehoboam king of Judah.**

*Whereupon the king took counsel, and made two calves
of gold, and said unto them, It is too much for you to
go up to Jerusalem: behold thy gods, O Israel, which
brought thee up out of the land of Egypt.*

**And he set the one in Bethel, and the other put he in
Dan.**

**And this thing became a sin: for the people went to
worship before the one, even unto Dan.**

**And he made an house of high places, and made priests
of the lowest of the people, which were not of the sons
of Levi.**

**And Jeroboam ordained a feast in the eighth month, on
the fifteenth day of the month, like unto the feast that
is in Judah, and he offered upon the altar. So did he
in Bethel, sacrificing unto the calves that he had made:
and he placed in Bethel the priests of the high places
which he had made.**

1 Kings 12:26-32

Will You Remember God?

Sometimes, you wonder if Christians can stand to be blessed. Can they ever handle the blessings that God has? I remember a Christian brother who was elevated to the high offices of government. The Lord blessed him with prosperity and power.

My first contact with him was several years before when we had a crusade in one of the cities of Ghana. We had to relate with him because he was the president of the Scripture Union fellowship of that town. We had to borrow some equipment from him. I remember how he came for the crusade and I remember his attitude. We felt like immature zealots in his presence. We wilted under his strict, moral, Christian eyes!

Years later, whilst watching television, I noticed that he had been promoted to one of the highest political positions in the country. I said to myself, "Wow, a Christian is deep into politics... ! I hope he can stay on course with the Lord." But that was not to be. The years went by and this fellow backslid terribly. It became apparent that he had put aside his faith.

Unfortunately, he also became ill and died suddenly. One day, I spoke to a pastor who ministered to him before he died. This pastor told me how this Christian politician had come to his house in the middle of the night demanding that the gate be opened to him. The Christian politician was now terminally ill and knew he was dying. He had come to see the pastor in the middle of the night because he could not breathe and he could not sleep.

He confessed his sins to the pastor and told him how he had forsaken his Christian wife and gone after other women. He cried and told the pastor how politics had even led him into occultism. Sitting in the pastor's home at one o'clock in the morning, he wept sore and asked for forgiveness for forsaking God. Alas, this man died a few days later. When I heard this story, I marvelled and considered how people forget their Christian commitment when they are elevated in this life.

Such was the story of Jeroboam who was picked from nowhere and elevated to the throne. He forgot the God who had picked him up and placed him on the throne. Unfortunately, Jeroboam disobeyed God at the first opportunity.

Paul declared that he knew how to stay close to God whilst poor and also when rich. This is the secret that Christians seem to lack - how to remember God when they are promoted.

Paul said,

I know how to get along with humble means, and I also know how to live in prosperity; in any and every circumstance I have learned the secret of being filled and going hungry, both of having abundance and suffering need.

Philippians 4:12, NASB

3. PEOPLE WHO FORGET BECOME PROUD.

Then David returned to bless his household. And Michal the daughter of Saul came out to meet David, and said, how glorious was the king of Israel to day, who uncovered himself to day in the eyes of the handmaids of his servants, as one of the vain fellows shamelessly uncovereth himself!

And David said unto Michal, It was before the LORD, which chose me before thy father, and before all his house, to appoint me ruler over the people of the LORD, over Israel: therefore will I play before the LORD.

2 Samuel 6:20-21

Sadly, many people forget how they came to be in privileged positions. However, this was not one of David's problems. He always remembered where the Lord had lifted him from. He knew that he was a "nobody" picked from looking after sheep and lifted to the throne of Israel. This made him grateful and worshipful even when his kingship was established.

Ousted Politicians

Unfortunately, many Christians forget where they came from.

I have needed help from the government on many occasions. Sadly, these powerful politicians had no time for an insignificant priest like me. Even Christians forget their heritage and place politics above their Christian faith. An interesting development, however, has been the turnaround in attitude by some of these people after leaving office.

Somehow, these politicians seem not to "know" you when they are in power. Yet they become so chummy and friendly when they are out of office and have lost their glory. A true friend is someone who will remember you when he is up there. Sadly, most people forget others when they are blessed.

I have had powerless past politicians ringing me up and chatting with me as though we were the fondest of friends. They called me by my first name and claimed that we were the best of buddies.

When I have met them on flights and in other settings I always got the same response. I have been invited to lunches and dinners by unseated politicians.

I never honoured any of these invitations because I did not regard these people as genuine friends. If they were genuine friends they would remember me when they were in the pomp and splendour of their offices.

God has shown me that there is no need to suck up to pretentious politicians. He will take care of His work with or without their help.

David said moreover, The LORD that delivered me out of the paw of the lion, and out of the paw of the bear, he will deliver me out of the hand of this Philistine. And Saul said unto David, Go, and the LORD be with thee.
1 Samuel 17:37

4. PEOPLE WHO FORGET CAN EASILY GET DIVORCED.

Unfortunately, many people forget the words they spoke to each other during their marriage ceremony.

"Till death us do part," they say boldly.

They declare, "For better or for worse."

Others vow, "In prosperity and in adversity we shall live together."

Many pronounce, "Many waters cannot quench our love. Neither can the floods drown our devotion."

They assert, "If any man will break up this union, it will be Satan."

Yet many of us try to break up this union. We have forgotten that we said that it would be Satan who would attempt to break up the union. Does this mean that if you try to break up your marriage you are Satan? Forgive!

Forgetting what you have said can go against you greatly. Most couples do not remember what they said to each other. Many wives forget how they proclaimed, "From this day forward, I shall love you and I shall give myself to you." Years later, when they are in bed with their husbands, they forget how they said, "I shall give myself to you."

Now, they do not give themselves to their husbands.

When they exchange rings, they say, "Let this ring be a symbol of our love for eternity." Unfortunately, the ring has become a symbol of sadness, bondage and quarrels.

One of the main reasons for divorce is forgetting what we said to each other. Most of the time the promises are made in our youth. By our middle age, we have forgotten what we said in our youth.

God is against those who do not remember what they said in their youth. The Bible refers to the wife as the "wife of your youth". In other words, she is the woman you liked when you were young, zealous and full of love. The Scripture urges you to remember the words of your covenant.

Yet you say, "For what reason?" Because the LORD has been a witness between you and the wife of your youth, against whom you have dealt treacherously, though she is your companion and your wife by covenant.

But not one has done so who has a remnant of the Spirit. And what did that one do while he was seeking a godly offspring? Take heed then to your spirit, and let no one deal treacherously against the wife of your youth.

For I hate divorce, says the LORD, the God of Israel, "and him who covers his garment with wrong," says the LORD of hosts. "So take heed to your spirit, that you do not deal treacherously."

Malachi 2:14-16, NASB

5. PEOPLE WHO FORGET BECOME PRESUMPTUOUS.

And Moses said unto Korah, Hear, I pray you, ye sons of Levi:

SEEMETH IT BUT A SMALL THING UNTO YOU, THAT THE GOD OF ISRAEL HATH SEPARATED YOU FROM THE CONGREGATION OF ISRAEL, TO BRING YOU NEAR to himself to do the service of the tabernacle of the LORD, and to stand before the congregation to minister unto them?

Numbers 16:8-9

The rebellion of Korah is of particular note because Moses rebuked Korah for his presumption. Presumption is "the arrogant assumption of privilege". When a person becomes presumptuous, he is too confident in a way that shows a lack of respect.

When people are fortunate to occupy certain positions, they often do not realize what a privilege they have. Moses recognized this sin in Korah.

Korah had the privilege of being a Levite and a leader of the congregation. Yet he spoke the rudest words to Moses, the servant of God.

They assembled together against Moses and Aaron, and said to them, "You have gone far enough, for all the congregation are holy, every one of them, and the Lord is in their midst; so why do you exalt yourselves above the assembly of the Lord?"

Numbers 16:3, NASB

Moses asked him whether he did not cherish the honoured position of a leader. He asked him, *"Seemeth it a small thing to you?"* I realize how people consider privileges as small things. They take them for granted and speak rudely to people who are way above them. This rude speaking is the cardinal sign of the presumptive spirit.

The Confident Pastor

Years ago, I noticed a brother who had the potential for being in the ministry. His pastor did not recognize his calling, but I did. In fact, his pastor told me personally that he was amazed that I could think of making somebody like that into a pastor. But I gave him an opportunity to be in the ministry. Then I trained him and appointed him as a pastor.

After some years, this brother became established in the ministry. Then one day, he dropped a bombshell and told us that he was leaving. He left our church, planted a church nearby, persistently invited our church members to leave us and join him; and virtually built his church by dividing ours. Soon, his new church consisted of many of our former members who had "migrated" to his new church. As you can imagine, this led to some conflict.

I had several exchanges with this fellow, some of which were not pleasant. One day, during one of our exchanges, he pointed out to me that what I was complaining about was unavoidable and that he could not help it if our church members were being attracted to his new church (which he had planted not far from ours). In other words, I needed to cure my insecurities!

This dear pastor pointed out to me that I myself had planted churches all over the place without apparent regard for their closeness to other churches. He also pointed out to me that I had started churches with people who were members of other churches.

He went on and put a direct question to me, "Why do you contradict yourself?"

Then he advised me to come to terms with the realities of pastors leaving my church; otherwise I would fight with everyone that ever left.

I was amazed as he continued, "You appointed me as a pastor and I honoured that appointment with my sweat and money. I owe you nothing further." He finally warned me saying, "I hold you personally responsible for anything that happens to my marriage."

He Forgot but I Remembered

I thought over these sayings for a long time. I considered how prosperous and wealthy he had become over the years and how he confidently rebuked and advised me today.

But I also remembered how years ago this brother (who was now rebuking me) was an impoverished, illegal immigrant who could not afford his own lunch. Now it seemed a small thing to him to have been lifted from his former state to where he currently was.

He could not remember his starting point; that is why he spoke confidently and in a way that showed a lack of respect (presumption).

You see, we all start from humble beginnings. I started my life and ministry from a very low point. What matters is not how low your starting point was. What matters is how well you can remember your lowly starting point! I realized that this brother had forgotten that he might never have become a pastor if he had not met me.

Perhaps, he had forgotten how I encouraged him to go into the ministry.

It seems he had forgotten how I chose him and sent him to a particular country, which he knew not.

He had forgotten that he would never have had the wife he had if I had not told her to marry him.

I remembered when his wife asked me about him. She did not want to marry, and especially she did not want to marry him.

But I convinced her and told her that he was a good person. Before he married her, I had such authority over his wife and she would have done anything I told her. In those days, the words and advice I gave to her were like the oracles of God. Whatever I said was what mattered.

Through his marriage which I sponsored, this brother had now become a member of a well-known family and enjoyed the privileges, financial wealth and inheritance of that family.

It seemed that all these had been forgotten by this brother who now said he owed me nothing!

Perhaps I would have to join Paul in saying, "I do not say to thee how thou owest unto me even thine own self besides." This brother said that he owed me nothing. But Paul said to Philemon that he owed him his very life.

I Paul have written it with mine own hand, I will repay it: albeit I do not say to thee how THOU OWEST UNTO ME EVEN THINE OWN SELF besides.
Philemon 19

It is always interesting to watch the sons of Korah rebuke their fathers. They love to put the fathers in their place. It seems a small thing to them. All that their fathers have done for them seems to them like nothing.

It is only because people forget where they were and who they were that they speak great swelling words of arrogance. Please do not repeat these errors. They are written for our example.

And Moses said unto Korah, Hear, I pray you, ye sons of Levi: Seemeth it but a small thing unto you, that the God of Israel hath separated you from the congregation of Israel, to bring you near to himself to do the service of the tabernacle of the LORD, and to stand before the congregation to minister unto them?

Numbers 16:8-9

6.   PEOPLE WHO FORGET BECOME REBELLIOUS.

And Samuel said, When thou wast LITTLE IN THINE OWN SIGHT, wast thou not made the head of the tribes of Israel, and the LORD anointed thee king over Israel?

1 Samuel 15:17

Saul did not remember to obey the Lord when he was lifted up. Samuel reminded him that he was nobody when God called and anointed him. Apparently, he had forgotten how little he was at the beginning.

The Wind is against You

People rebel against those who set them up because they do not remember how they came to be where they are. I remember a brother who rebelled against his General Superintendent. He was sent to a foreign country to plant a church. After the church grew and became successful, this brother decided to dissociate himself from the church that sent him. I visited the General Superintendent and he spoke bitterly about this missionary.

47

I was amazed to hear that this brother had written him a nasty letter telling him to back off his ministry.

He told his pastor that he owed him *nothing* and that he had done *nothing* for him.

The General Superintendent was very angry as he narrated the story of this ungrateful and forgetful son.

As we talked, he said, "This fellow was one of my house boys (domestic servants) who I raised up." Then he pointed to the ground and showed me the spot where this fellow would pray along with some others.

"This fellow belonged to a group of nobodies I helped.

I welcomed them into my house and gave them a place to pray in my living room. I trained them in the ministry," he said.

He described how he had used his influence to get visas for this young man (in Africa, it is a miracle to obtain a visa for a European country when you do not have a substantial or wealthy background).

Then he lifted his fingers and cursed the man, *"The wind is against him."*

Because this boy had forgotten where he came from and who had helped him, he received a curse that night.

One day, a year later, I happened to see this forgetful minister in a shopping mall. He had gone shopping with his wife and had filled his trolley with saucepans, frying pans and other household items. He was living happily ever after with his wife, far away from his angry General Superintendent.

As soon as I saw him, I remembered the fingers that were lifted up and the curse that *the wind was against him.*

And it came to pass that the wind was indeed against him! As time went by, the wind dismantled his church and his congregation scattered! I would meet his prized members and financiers and they would tell me they were no more with him.

This same wind blew him into adultery and obviously destroyed his marriage. The wind continued to blow until it had blown away his wife and children. The wind blew him out of the country to which he had been sent. The wind blew him over the seas and far away into obscurity. This is the wind that blows the forgetful and rebellious ones away!

7. PEOPLE WHO FORGET BECOME SECOND-RATE MINISTERS.

Remembering what you have been through greatly improves your preaching and writing skills. Many people are boring preachers because they never give us real life accounts of what God has taken them through.

It is the ability to *remember* that makes the difference between a good preacher and a bad one. You will be surprised at how attentive the congregation becomes when you start to tell them a real life story.

The Apostle Paul remembered his experiences in great detail. He would often tell the stories to anyone who would listen. In his letters, he described his background in great detail. He narrated his experiences and even remembered the different emotions of each season.

Paul Tells Agrippa about the Damascus Road Experience

And as I punished them often in all the synagogues, I tried to force them to blaspheme; and being furiously enraged at them, I kept pursuing them even to foreign cities.

While so engaged as I was journeying to Damascus with the authority and commission of the chief priests, at midday, O King, I saw on the way a light from heaven, brighter than the sun, shining all around me and those who were journeying with me.

And when we had all fallen to the ground, I heard a voice saying to me in the Hebrew dialect, "Saul, Saul, why are you persecuting Me? It is hard for you to kick against the goads."

And I said, "Who are You, Lord?" And the Lord said, "I am Jesus whom you are persecuting."

Acts 26:11-15, NASB

Paul Tells the Galatians about His Early Ministry

But when God, who had set me apart even from my mother's womb and called me through His grace, was pleased to reveal His Son in me so that I might preach Him among the Gentiles, I did not immediately consult with flesh and blood, nor did I go up to Jerusalem to those who were apostles before me; but I went away to Arabia, and returned once more to Damascus.

Then three years later I went up to Jerusalem to become acquainted with Cephas, and stayed with him fifteen days.

Galatians 1:15-18 (NASB)

Paul Tells the Philippians about His Upbringing

Although I myself might have confidence even in the flesh. If anyone else has a mind to put confidence in the flesh, I far more: circumcised the eighth day, of the nation of Israel, of the tribe of Benjamin, a Hebrew of Hebrews; as to the Law, a Pharisee; as to zeal, a persecutor of the church; as to the righteousness which is in the Law, found blameless.

But whatever things were gain to me, those things I have counted as loss for the sake of Christ.

Philippians 3:4-7 (NASB)

Paul Tells the Corinthians about His Personal Problems

Are they servants of Christ? - I speak as if insane - I more so; in far more labors, in far more imprisonments, beaten times without number, often in danger of death.

Five times I received from the Jews thirty-nine lashes.

50

Three times I was beaten with rods, once I was stoned, three times I was shipwrecked, a night and a day I have spent in the deep.

I have been on frequent journeys, in dangers from rivers, dangers from robbers, dangers from my countrymen, dangers from the Gentiles, dangers in the city, dangers in the wilderness, dangers on the sea, dangers among false brethren; I have been in labor and hardship, through many sleepless nights, in hunger and thirst, often without food, in cold and exposure."

2 Corinthians 11:23-27, NASB

Paul Tells the Corinthians about His Feelings

For we do not want you to be unaware, brethren, of our affliction which came to us in Asia, that we were burdened excessively, beyond our strength, so that we despaired even of life; indeed, we had the sentence of death within ourselves so that we would not trust in ourselves, but in God who raises the dead; who delivered us from so great a peril of death, and will deliver us, He on whom we have set our hope. And He will yet deliver us,

2 Corinthians 1:8-10, NASB

Become a better preacher! Remember your life's experiences and share them! Do not think that your life is uneventful and boring. Do not think that you have no interesting life experiences to share. That is a deception.

Begin to remember and talk about the little things that God has brought you through. I promise you; your ministry will come alive and your preaching will be anointed!

8. PEOPLE WHO FORGET LACK THE COMPASSION NEEDED FOR MINISTRY.

But when he saw the multitudes, he was moved with compassion on them, because they fainted, and were scattered abroad, as sheep having no shepherd.

Matthew 9:36

The story of the Good Samaritan illustrates this reality. I am certain that forgetfulness leads to a lack of passion for true ministry.

Levites and priests passed by filled with the knowledge of God. But they did not have *compassion*. When the man with *compassion* came by, he was moved and saved the brother who was half-dead. This world is half-dead, waiting for us to come and save them. We have the Gospel of Jesus Christ, the only hope of this world!

> **But a certain Samaritan, as he journeyed, came where he was: and when he saw him, he had COMPASSION on him,**
>
> **And went to him, and bound up his wounds, pouring in oil and wine, and set him on his own beast, and brought him to an inn, and took care of him.**
>
> **And on the morrow when he departed, he took out two pence, and gave them to the host, and said unto him, Take care of him; and whatsoever thou spendest more, when I come again, I will repay thee.**
>
> **Which now of these three, thinkest thou, was neighbour unto him that fell among the thieves?**
>
> **Luke 10:33-36**

The modern inventions of television, radio, cassettes, CDs and the internet have made Scripture more available than ever before. Sadly, the increase of Scripture and the availability of this knowledge have not resulted in more of God's compassion. The compassion for souls is almost absent whilst the love for treasures and finances is at its peak!

The sad reality is that the evangelization of this world will not be accomplished without compassion. But how can we have compassion when we do not remember what it is like to almost go to Hell?

Paul Remembered

Brethren, my heart's desire and prayer to God for Israel is, that they might be saved.

Romans 10:1

The Apostle Paul was moved with compassion because he remembered people who were just like him. He remembered his own relatives who lived in darkness. He remembered how he was almost not saved himself. At a point, he wished he could kill himself so that they would be saved. "I say the truth in Christ, I lie not, my conscience also bearing me witness in the Holy Ghost, That I have great heaviness and continual sorrow in my heart.

For I could wish that myself were accursed from Christ for my brethren, my kinsmen according to the flesh" (Romans 9:1-3).

Having the kind of compassion needed for ministry goes along with the ability to *remember.* People have no compassion because they do not remember.

One day, I met a millionaire who had established a large prisons ministry.

He told me how he had been thrown into prison for several years and then had been released miraculously. After being released, this man could not forget his experience in the prison.

The Lord used him to establish a nationwide prison ministry, which touched the lives of thousands of prisoners.

God expects you not to forget what you have seen, heard and experienced.

Chapter 5

Seven Keys That Will Help You Remember

1. STUDY HISTORY.

There are certain reasons why people forget things. You must fight the natural tendency to forget important things. As the children of Israel prepared to experience the Promised Land, God knew that they would forget almost every important thing they had learned. Moses narrated and rehearsed the history of their journey to them.

Let History Keep You from Forgetting

Now there arose up a new king over Egypt, which knew not Joseph.

Exodus 1:8

Pharaoh forgot the history of his own country. He did not know that his country would have been wiped out if it had not been for the good works of Joseph.

Yet, he forgot who the Israelites were and began to persecute them. Perhaps if he had read his history book, he would not have persecuted Joseph's descendants. He repaid the good that Joseph had done to the nation of Egypt with evil.

Pharaoh's Expensive Forgetfulness

Pharaoh's failure to read history cost him dearly. By being ungrateful to the Israelites, he sowed the seeds of the destruction of Egypt. God stepped in and wiped out the economy of Egypt. He destroyed their farms, their infrastructure, their water, their cattle, their vegetation and their personal comforts.

I think that history is one of the most important subjects ever to be studied. Please read your history books! Please read biographies of men of God. In them you will find great lessons of life which must never be forgotten.

2. DO NOT LET YOUR SUCCESSES DESTROY YOUR MEMORY.

But thou shalt REMEMBER the LORD thy God: for it is he that giveth thee power to get wealth, that he may establish his covenant which he sware unto thy fathers, as it is this day.

Deuteronomy 8:18

Moses defined success as "when thou hast eaten and art full".

Successful people suffer most from a lack of remembrance. They cannot remember how they came to be where they are. Like the prophet he was, Moses warned them about specific blessings and the tendency to forget the Lord's input into their lives.

When thou hast eaten and art full, then thou shalt bless the LORD thy God for the good land which he hath given thee.
Beware that thou forget not the LORD thy God, in not keeping his commandments, and his judgments, and his statutes, which I command thee this day:
Lest when thou hast eaten and art full, and hast built goodly houses, and dwelt therein;
And when thy herds and thy flocks multiply, and thy silver and thy gold is multiplied, and all that thou hast is multiplied;
Then thine heart be lifted up, and thou forget the LORD thy God, which brought thee forth out of the land of Egypt, from the house of bondage;

Deuteronomy 8:10-14

Everyone who has built goodly houses and dwelt therein should be careful of forgetting the Lord.

Everyone whose money (silver and gold) is multiplied should be careful of forgetting the Lord.

55

Everyone who has prospered is a candidate for pride and neglect of the Lord.

Do not ask me to explain how this problem comes about.

It is just a known fact that blessings and prosperity make people forget God. That is why it is easier for a camel to pass through the eye of a needle than for a rich man to enter the kingdom of God.

What must you do about it?

Just decide to be extra God-fearing and extra spiritual when you have all these things.

Pray for humility and grace to avoid this all-too-familiar trend!

3. DO NOT LET THE PASSAGE OF TIME MAKE YOU FORGET.

Yet did not the chief butler REMEMBER Joseph, but forgat him.

Genesis 40:23

Another reason why people forget is simply the passage of time. When the chief butler was in prison, he was helped greatly by Joseph. But he forgot Joseph when he was released. Even though he had been helped in prison, he forgot about Joseph in his freedom.

I have watched how people forget where they came from. As the years have gone by, they need to be reminded of their beginnings.

At different times, the Lord used me to start different fellowships, groups and churches. Sometimes I would hand over the group to a leader and leave them for some time. Invariably, they forgot me. They forgot how they began and they forgot about me. With the passage of time, they did not even want my involvement anymore.

I remember one particular fellowship I started and allowed to run for some time. Later on, I came back to them and explained that I wanted to take up the leadership of the group again. After a series of discussions, I sensed that my leadership was not welcome anymore so I abandoned the idea. I reflected on the turn of events. As I thought over the situation, I considered how people easily forget where they come from.

These people had forgotten that they did not even know each other before I had pulled them together and introduced them to one another. In addition, they had forgotten that none of them had had a vision for such a fellowship. I had the vision and invited them to participate.

Also, they had forgotten that all the activities they currently engaged in were things that I had instituted. They had forgotten how associating with me had led them to enjoy the relationships they now cherished.

But such is the lot of a founder. He must be prepared to be forgotten and set aside. This is the reason why people hold on to leadership positions until they die. They fear to hand over their prized vision to men who forget. The butler forgot Joseph. Many people forget those who have been real spiritual blessings to them.

4. RECOGNIZE THE HAND OF GOD IN EVERYTHING THAT HAPPENS.

But hast lifted up thyself against the Lord of heaven; and they have brought the vessels of his house before thee, and thou, and thy lords, thy wives, and thy concubines, have drunk wine in them; and thou hast praised the gods of silver, and gold, of brass, iron, wood, and stone, which see not, nor hear, nor know: and THE GOD IN WHOSE HAND THY BREATH IS, AND WHOSE ARE ALL THY WAYS, HAST THOU NOT GLORIFIED:

Daniel 5:23

Many people do not understand *why* or *how* they are blessed. They just enjoy the blessings but do not understand how they are acquired.

For instance, most Africans do not know how Europe was built. They have no idea how a clean and orderly society is created. They love to go to these Western countries and live there if possible.

But they do things that destroy their own nations. They fight against the very things that create what they want. They oppose decisions that will bring order, cleanliness and all the other things that the Western world has.

They reject the practical kind of leaders that can create the Western type of environments and choose impractical, ceremonial and handsome men who know little about leadership!

They simply do not understand how clean, orderly, modern and wealthy societies are created.

Many do not understand how leadership works. I have concluded that most people just choose the wrong leader. They simply do not know the type of leadership qualities that are needed to take us out of squalor. The radical, strong leaders who are needed to move large populations of undeveloped societies into prosperity are simply not chosen through elections.

Often, smooth talking, "please everyone," traditional and "nice" people are chosen by undeveloped societies because the people like their approach. Unfortunately, such people do not bring true advancement.

Similarly, Christians do not know how they come to be blessed. Many believers do not understand why certain things even happen. They forget that God holds their destiny in His hands.

... But you have not praised the God who gives you the breath of life and controls your destiny!
Daniel 5:23-24 TLB

Belshazzar praised the gods of gold and of silver, wood and stone. But he did not honour the God who had really lifted him up. The prophet Daniel rebuked Belshazzar for not remembering the One who really mattered.

He holds our breath in His hand and He controls all our ways. He therefore is the source of all our blessings.

How can we forget the one who controls everything about our lives? We cannot live a day longer than He allows. We cannot do anything that He does not allow. He's got the whole world in His hands. We must not forget the hand of God which rules in our affairs.

5. CONTINUALLY RECOGNIZE THE PEOPLE GOD HAS USED IN YOUR LIFE.

And Laban said unto him, I pray thee, if I have found favour in thine eyes, tarry: for I have learned by experience that THE LORD HATH BLESSED ME FOR THY SAKE.

Genesis 30:27

People forget because they do not recognize God's vessel. They do not realize that they are where they are because God blessed them through their association with someone. A failure to understand this is the cause of many of life's disasters.

It takes humility to recognize that God has chosen certain people, given them a call and favoured all those who help their cause. God chose Israel and has blessed all those who help that nation. There is nothing you can do about God's choices.

Laban was a wise unbeliever who recognized that his blessings had come by associating with Jacob. He did not want to part company with Jacob because he sensed that the blessing came by this association.

When the Ark of the Covenant was in the house of Obededom, everything flourished. The house of Obededom was fully blessed because of the presence of the Ark of the Covenant.

59

And it was told king David, saying, The LORD hath blessed the house of Obed-edom, and all that pertaineth unto him, because of the ark of God...

2 Samuel 6:12

A wise and spiritual person will attach himself to people who are recognizably called and favoured by the Lord. What you need is to tap into some of the grace given to that person. People forget how they were lifted from the depths to great heights by relating with a particular person.

Two Forgetful Associates

I remember the pastor of a five thousand member church who had two powerful associates. These associate ministers forgot how their destinies had changed by associating with their senior pastor.

One day, their senior pastor, sensing the mounting rebellion transferred these two associates away from himself.

I met one of these associates and he spoke bitterly of his transfer.

He said, "Even that the word 'transfer' was applied to me is preposterous."

The other associate, who was equally bitter, said many derogatory things about his senior pastor.

I knew it was a matter of time before they would both resign. A few months later, they both left the ministry and dissociated from their senior pastor.

The years went by and I watched how their lives evolved. The senior pastor continued to go from strength to strength and his ministry became the largest in the city. Sadly, though, the associates seemed to wither away.

One of them tried to start a church, but could not get more than five members to join him. His church never grew out of the living room of his home.

The other became a pastor of another church, but was dismissed soon after for bad behaviour.

Both of these associates continued to struggle for years moving from one job to another and never amounting to anything.

I realized that these associates had moved out of their place and had not recognized how God had blessed them through association. Of course it takes humility to even recognize this truth.

Do not be afraid of acknowledging that God has used a man to change your life!

6. GROW IN YOUR UNDERSTANDING OF WHY GOD BLESSES PEOPLE.

When you do not *understand* why God blesses someone, you will quickly neglect the important principles he lives by. *A deeper understanding helps you to have a better memory.* That is why teaching deploys various techniques to induce a greater understanding of issues. The more you understand, the more you remember! An ancient Chinese proverb says, "You hear you forget; you see you remember; you do you understand."

Why King David was Blessed by God

Perhaps King Solomon did not understand why God had blessed his father David. King Solomon remembered how God had been angry with his father for sleeping with somebody's wife and decided to avoid falling into his father's sins. Probably, this is why he married so many women. He did not want to commit adultery so he decided to marry every girl he saw. In the end, he had married one thousand women! This in itself is a miracle.

Maybe Solomon did not understand that David was ultimately a man after God's own heart who would never worship an idol. David wholly and passionately served God in spite of his human failings.

You may think that God was displeased with Solomon because of the numerous women he loved. Although these numerous women in his life caused problems, this was not the reason why God rejected Solomon.

The Bible tells us clearly that God rejected Solomon because he was not devoted to the Lord and worshipped idols in his old age. King David never worshipped idols and there was no mention of any such thing during his time.

> **For when Solomon was old, his wives turned his heart away after other gods; and his heart was not wholly devoted to the LORD his God, as the heart of David his father had been.**
>
> **1 Kings 11:4, NASB**

The real secret behind King David's blessing was his wholehearted service to the living God. Perhaps, not understanding the secret behind someone's success will lead you to set aside the very thing which made him great.

7. DO NOT HAVE A REBELLIOUS BLACKOUT.

> **If thou count me therefore a partner, receive him as myself. If he hath wronged thee, or oweth thee ought, put that on mine account; I Paul have written it with mine own hand, I will repay it: albeit I DO NOT SAY TO THEE HOW THOU OWEST UNTO ME EVEN THINE OWN SELF BESIDES.**
>
> **Philemon 17-19**

Paul, like many fathers and apostles, would not bother to tell the young ones that they actually owed their entire lives to him. Philemon did not just owe him gratitude for some nice teachings. Philemon did not just owe him gratitude for some powerful prayers. He owed his very life to him! One day, Paul decided to point this out to Philemon because he was asking for a favour.

There are people who rebel against authority and therefore need to wipe out the memory of those who have helped them. When people do not want to show gratitude, they consciously black out the memory of good things done for them.

They selectively retain the things they want to remember and delete the memory of other things. They then try to attribute their success to other reasons, minimizing any reference to the one who actually helped them.

They say things like, *"I would have been here anyway. I would have been in the ministry anyway. I would have been ordained anyway. I would have had a better life elsewhere. I would have travelled to these countries anyway."*

They also say things like, *"I cannot say thank you forever. I have honoured you enough."*

But Paul told Philemon, "You owe me your whole life besides." You see, there are things that affect all aspects of your life. The receiving of salvation is not just the receiving of a good teaching. It is the rescuing of an entire life!

To be in the ministry is not just another opportunity to occupy some social position. It is the highest privilege that can be given to a human being with unimaginable eternal rewards! There is nothing higher than working for the King of Kings.

Because of the Anointing

One day, I was in Tulsa, Oklahoma attending a Winter Bible Seminar. At a point in the programme, the Lord told me to give an offering to Brother Hagin. I did not have a problem with that, so I agreed.

That night, Kenneth Hagin spoke about many things and told us how many million dollars he had earned that year. He also spoke about other financial blessings he had received from the Lord. When I heard his testimony, I became discouraged when I thought of the size of the offering I had for him. I then decided not to give him the offering at all. After all, I was sure that he did not need my money!

But in the morning, the Lord rebuked me severely about this and told me that I was ungrateful. He showed me that even though I had never spoken to Kenneth Hagin or received any physical benefit from him directly, all the blessings of my life had come through the anointing I had received through him.

He told me that I had received an anointing through the ministry of Kenneth Hagin.

He then pointed out to me that everything I did in the ministry was related to that anointing and therefore to Kenneth Hagin.

He told me that the house that I lived in was because of the anointing that He had given me.

He told me that the cars I had were available to me because of the anointing I had received through Kenneth Hagin.

He showed me that all the money I had was because of the ministry and anointing I had received through Kenneth Hagin. He also showed me that my ability to buy a ticket and fly to Tulsa, Oklahoma from Africa was due to the anointing I had received through this man. My whole life was related to the anointing that came through one man.

Why Did I Want to Hold Back?

Why did I not want to give him an offering? What reason could there be to withhold an offering from him? What was I thinking about? Could I not see that everything was related to this person?

"When would you have such a chance again," the Lord asked me. I wept like a baby as He rebuked me about this.

Sometimes we want to black out the reality of how we owe everything to a particular person. We do not want to attribute all the great things of our life to one person. However, there is no need to black out the reality of what God has done.

Never forget that many things are often related to one individual. Be grateful to God and to whoever He has used to bless you. This is what Paul meant when he said to Philemon, "I don't want to remind you do I, that YOU OWE YOUR VERY LIFE TO ME" (Philemon 19, The Message Bible).

Chapter 6

Things That Righteous People Remember

1. RIGHTEOUS PEOPLE REMEMBER IMPORTANT ANNIVERSARIES.

Thou shalt eat no leavened bread with it; seven days shalt thou eat unleavened bread therewith, even the bread of affliction; for thou camest forth out of the land of Egypt in haste: that thou mayest REMEMBER THE DAY WHEN THOU CAMEST FORTH OUT OF THE LAND OF EGYPT all the days of thy life.

Deuteronomy 16:3

Most people just remember their birthdays. But there are days that are more important than your birthday. The day you were born again, the day you were filled with the Spirit, the day you were healed, and the day you were called to the ministry.

What about the day you came out of a near-death experience?

What about the day someone helped you out of a critical situation?

What about the day someone introduced you to an important person?

What about the day you were helped and the day of your promotion?

And what about the day Jesus was born, the day He died and the day He rose from the dead?

These are important days for Christians to remember.

2. PEOPLE WHO ARE RIGHTEOUS REMEMBER THEIR LOW POINTS AND HOW THEY CAME OUT OF THEM.

And REMEMBER THAT THOU WAST A SERVANT IN THE LAND OF EGYPT, and that the LORD thy God brought thee out thence through a mighty hand and by a stretched out arm: therefore the LORD thy God commanded thee to keep the Sabbath day.

Deuteronomy 5:15

People who are righteous remember exactly who helped them out of their low points.

In this Scripture, the Lord emphasizes that He brought them out of the land of Egypt. It is easy to ascribe honour to someone who didn't really help you.

Now that you have prospered, you can easily say, "I would have had it any way." It is easy to forget people who helped you at critical moments of your life.

As the years go by, the critical moments fade from your memory and you forget how vulnerable you were at a point in time. God did not want the Israelites to forget how vulnerable they were in the land of Egypt and how He saved them in that moment.

Then beware lest thou forget the Lord, which brought thee forth out of the land of Egypt, from the house of bondage.

Deuteronomy 6:12

3. PEOPLE WHO REMEMBER ARE ABLE TO OVERCOME THEIR FEARS.

THOU SHALT NOT BE AFRAID OF THEM: BUT SHALT WELL REMEMBER what the LORD thy God did unto Pharaoh, and unto all Egypt;

Deuteronomy 7:18

People who do not remember are filled with fear. If you remember what the Lord has done for you through the years you will be filled with faith. You will know that all things are possible! You will know that He can do it again.

When you forget the great things that the Lord has done, all kinds of irrational fears grip your heart. Those fears can lead you on a journey of destruction.

4. PEOPLE WHO ARE RIGHTEOUS REMEMBER THE COMMANDMENTS OF THE LORD.

Beware that thou forget not the Lord thy God, in NOT KEEPING HIS COMMANDMENTS, and his judgments, and his statutes, which I command thee this day:

Deuteronomy 8:11

A good employee always takes a notebook and starts writing when the boss starts speaking. Why does a good employee write things down? Everybody forgets instructions they don't write down. If you do not make the extra effort you will soon forget things the Lord has asked you to do.

God will speak to you through His servants. There are special words or phrases that must stay in your spirit. God will use those sentences to guide your life.

Beware of Voices of Haste

One day, a man of God facing a crisis was presented with an ultimatum. He was asked to resign from his position by signing an apparently harmless letter.

Under pressure, he decided to sign the letter and by that decision he inadvertently lost his entire ministry. Years later, he could not understand why he had done something as foolish as that.

He described how he had attended a conference as a younger preacher and heard a minister make a statement that had left an indelible impression on his heart and mind.

67

The statement was: "BEWARE VOICES OF HASTE."

This is a scriptural statement because the Bible says he that believeth shall not make haste (Isaiah 28:16). That statement had stuck in his spirit and he knew that it was an important word of wisdom for him. Somehow in the heat of his crisis he forgot that statement. Forgetting that statement cost him his ministry. If he had remembered these words, he would not have hastily signed that document and handed over his ministry to strangers.

This is why the Lord said, "You shall remember the words which the servant of the Lord commanded you." There are certain words spoken by God's servants that you must remember.

Righteous people remember what God tells them to remember even if it doesn't make sense. God asked the children of Israel not to forget what Amalek had done to them.

REMEMBER WHAT AMALEK DID UNTO THEE
by the way, when ye were come forth out of Egypt;
Deuteronomy 25:17

Remembering the wickedness of certain people may be important for your safety. Time has a way of erasing the memory of certain evils. There are relationships that will always be stumbling blocks to your life. There are relationships God wants you to stay away from both today and in the future.

That is why God wanted His people to remember what Amalek had done.

Forgetting Amalek is like forgetting all the potential dangers and killers of your ministry. "Therefore it shall be, when the Lord thy God hath given thee rest from all thine enemies round about, in the land which the Lord thy God giveth thee for an inheritance to possess it, that thou shalt BLOT OUT THE REMEMBRANCE OF AMALEK from under heaven; THOU SHALT NOT FORGET IT" (Deuteronomy 25:19).

5. RIGHTEOUS PEOPLE REMEMBER THE OLD DAYS.

REMEMBER THE DAYS OF OLD, consider the years of many generations: ask thy father, and he will shew thee; thy elders, and they will tell thee.

Deuteronomy 32:7

Young people often make the mistake of thinking that everything old is useless. Remembering the days of old is what we call studying history. I know of no subject that is more important than the study of history! History repeats itself in cycles!

Events just repeat themselves. History repeats itself. Studying history will help you know the future. The future is not determined by what you expect or by the principles you have put in place.

Lions have natural instincts that they follow mindlessly. Following these natural instincts create the cycles of lion life such as hunting, killing, mating and bringing forth cubs.

When human beings follow their instincts mindlessly, they create cycles and trends of their own. The trends of human life are difficult to predict except you study history.

Human history is determined more by man's jealousies, hatred, lust and malice than by anything else. These invisible "rivers" lead to certain patterns that are difficult to predict unless you study history.

A study of the history of man simply reveals a pattern of strife and war. People who watch the History Channel are amazed to find that much of man's history is simply wars that repeat themselves. History reveals that the surprising outcome of human instincts is strife and war.

Anyone who does not study history will be surprised at life.

This is why God's instruction is to remember the days of old.

6. RIGHTEOUS PEOPLE REMEMBER THE BENEFITS OF THE LORD.

Bless the LORD, O my soul, and FORGET NOT ALL HIS BENEFITS

Psalms 103:2

Why is it important to "forget" not all his benefits? It is important to see that the benefits are from the Lord. It is important to see that every good and perfect gift comes from above.

The ability to see and to remember the benefits of serving the Lord is necessary if we are to walk with Him.

When you don't remember benefits you become a murmurer. Evil spirits inhabit murmurers! Without the ability to remember benefits, discontentment sets in. Read your Bible and discover what happens to murmurers and complainers.

Forgetful people must never attempt to work for God in full-time ministry. There will be too many things to complain about. Full-time ministry is reserved for people who can see benefits, *remember* benefits and be *grateful* for the smallest benefits.

If you can remember that every benefit is from the Lord, you will have the right attitude when you are promoted. You will remember God when you are promoted! You will remember those who helped you when you are promoted! You will even remember those who suffered with you when you are promoted! The thief on the cross knew that Jesus would remember those who suffered with Him.

And he said unto Jesus, Lord, REMEMBER ME WHEN THOU COMEST INTO THY KINGDOM.

Luke 23:42

The thief on the cross knew that Jesus was just about to be promoted. He begged Jesus to remember him when the promotion came. Is this not what we pray for when our friends are lifted up? Jesus promised to put the thief in paradise.

Unfortunately, when an ordinary person is promoted through politics, marriage or football they do not remember the commoners anymore. Please remember us in the day you are promoted.

7. RIGHTEOUS PEOPLE REMEMBER WHAT GOD DOES TO PEOPLE JUST LIKE THEM.

Remember Lot's wife.

Luke 17:32

Remember what the Lord did to Lot's wife. Jesus urged His followers to remember Lot's wife. Lot's wife speaks of someone who looks backward instead of forward. She represents all who follow the Lord but whose hearts are somewhere else.

I have seen missionary wives who lived with their husbands on the mission field but whose hearts were not on the field. Lot's wife was looking back at where she came from. She wanted to go back. Lot's wife was a missionary's wife who wanted to go back home!

Lot's wife did not deserve to be among the few that were saved. That is why she turned into a pillar of salt. Every minister should remember Lot's wife. Every pastor's wife should remember Lot's wife. Every Christian should remember to serve the Lord without looking back.

Also remember what the Lord did to Miriam. Remember what happened to someone just like you!

Remember what the lord thy God did unto Miriam...

Deuteronomy 24:9

Whenever something happens to someone just like you, you must take note of it. It is a message from the Lord for you.

That could have been you but God spared you and chose to warn you instead. The Lord told the Israelites to remember what happened to Miriam. What happened to Miriam could happen to anyone.

8. RIGHTEOUS PEOPLE REMEMBER THE POOR AND THE PRISONERS.

Only *they would* that we should REMEMBER THE POOR; the same which I also was forward to do.

Galatians 2:10

You do not have to be urged to remember the rich. It is natural to remember those who are prominent amongst you.

The poor man, on the other hand, comes to you laden with problems and needs. He needs your help and he wants to get as much as he can from you. Most of us turn our eyes away from the endless needs of the poor. The Scripture is clear that poor people should be remembered and included in our plans.

Prisoners are part of our society but they are out of sight. It is also easy to forget them. It is easy to forget that they even exist. The Scripture tells us to remember the people in prison. Every church must have a prison ministry. Every pastor must preach in the prisons of his country.

Remember them that are in bonds, as bound with them; And them which suffer adversity, as being yourselves also in the body.

Hebrews 13:3

9. RIGHTEOUS PEOPLE REMEMBER GOD'S SERVANTS.

REMEMBER THEM WHICH HAVE THE RULE OVER YOU, who have spoken unto you the word of God: whose faith follow, considering the end of their conversation.

Hebrews 13:7

Now I praise you, brethren, that ye REMEMBER ME IN ALL THINGS, and keep the ordinances, as I delivered *them* to you.

1 Corinthians 11:2

We must also remember the servants of the Lord. Many church members have stable and normal lives because of the direction and inspiration they receive from their church. Yet the pastor is often the last to be remembered. Sometimes people speak of their new jobs, new contracts and salary increases. Often, all we see is a new car, a new house and more celebrations.

The pastor is often not considered in the new dispensation of prosperity. Actually, when he dares ask support for the ministry, he is told about the mortgages, the loans and the other bills that have to be paid.

The pastor is also informed about how certain contracts and payments have not yet materialized. He is then promised that he will be remembered when things work out. When people do support the ministry, they often do not support the pastor himself.

The righteous person will remember the pastor who labours spiritually for them.

10. RIGHTEOUS PEOPLE REMEMBER WHAT THEY HAVE RECEIVED.

REMEMBER THEREFORE HOW THOU HAST RECEIVED AND HEARD, and hold fast, and repent. If therefore thou shalt not watch, I will come on thee as a thief, and thou shalt not know what hour I will come upon thee.

Revelation 3:3

Sometimes we forget the different gifts that we have received. If God gave you five talents you will be judged for the use of all five. Many people have forgotten what they have received. Some of us have put aside our gifts. Some of us have trivialized certain gifts thinking them to be nothing.

A great prophet described a vision in which he saw the Lord. He told of how the Lord had rebuked him for not using the prophetic gift as much as he should have.

The Lord told him that his life would be shortened if he did not repent and use his gift. Remember what you have received because you will account for every single gift you were given.

73

Chapter 7

Seven Spiritual Effects of Remembrance

1. **REMEMBRANCE CAUSES A STIRRING OF THE BELIEVER.**

   This second epistle, beloved, I now write unto you; in both which I STIR UP YOUR PURE MINDS BY WAY OF REMEMBRANCE

   2 Peter 3:1

   Yea, I think it meet, as long as I am in this tabernacle, TO STIR YOU UP BY PUTTING YOU IN REMEMBRANCE

   2 Peter 1:13

Remembrance stirs up your spirit and spurs you on to good works. Powerful preaching that reminds us of our salvation stirs up Christians to soul winning. Powerful preaching that reminds us of Heaven and Hell stirs up Christians to soul winning.

Sit back and remember the things the Lord has told you. Sit back and remember your visions and dreams. Get excited again as you remember what God is going to do with you.

2. **REMEMBRANCE CAUSES PEOPLE TO BE ESTABLISHED.**

   Wherefore I will not be negligent to put you always in remembrance of these things, though ye know them, and BE ESTABLISHED IN THE PRESENT TRUTH.

   Yea, I think it meet, as long as I am in this tabernacle, to stir you up by putting you in remembrance; knowing that shortly I must put off this my tabernacle, even as our Lord Jesus Christ hath shewed me.

Moreover I will endeavour that ye may be able after my decease to have these things always in remembrance.

2 Peter 1:12-15

Peter wanted his followers to be established. He wrote this letter to them with this in mind.

Peter wanted to make sure that they would remember certain things after his death. That is why he wrote this letter.

Books, biographies and knowledge of history will make you remember and will establish you in your mission.

3. REMEMBRANCE MAKES PEOPLE GRATEFUL.

I thank my God upon every remembrance of you

Philippians 1:3

Paul became thankful when he remembered the Philippians. Remembrance and gratitude are related virtues. When you think of what Jesus has done for you your heart should be filled with gratitude. When you remember what someone has done for you become grateful for the person's life.

4. REMEMBRANCE CAUSES YOU TO RECEIVE THE HOLY COMMUNION.

And when he had given thanks, he brake it, and said, Take, eat: this is my body, which is broken for you: THIS DO IN REMEMBRANCE OF ME.

1 Corinthians 11:24

People give all sorts of reasons for the Holy Communion. But the main reason for the institution of the Lord's Supper is *remembrance*. Jesus, knowing how forgetful people were, instituted the celebration of the Holy Communion. He wanted people to remember His sacrifice for them.

5. REMEMBRANCE CAUSES YOU TO BE A DOER OF THE WORD.

But be ye doers of the word, and not hearers only, deceiving your own selves.

For if any be a hearer of the word, and not a doer, he is like unto a man beholding his natural face in a glass:

For he beholdeth himself, and goeth his way, and straightway forgetteth what manner of man he was.

James 1:22-24

When people do not remember the Word they become hearers and not doers of the Word. You must become a doer of the Word by remembering things that must not be forgotten. There are many hearers of the Word but not so many doers. It is time to become a doer of the Word.

6. REMEMBRANCE CAUSES YOU TO WORK QUICKLY WHILE YOU HAVE THE TIME.

For the living know that they shall die: but THE DEAD know not any thing, neither have they any more a reward; for THE MEMORY OF THEM IS FORGOTTEN.

Ecclesiastes 9:5

Because the dead are quickly forgotten, it is important to fulfil your ministry while you are alive. People will forget about you once you die. Do not think that much will be done when you are dead and gone. If you have anything you want to do, do it now.

7. REMEMBRANCE OF THE WRONG THINGS CAN PULL YOU BACKWARDS.

Brethren, I count not myself to have apprehended: but *THIS* ONE THING I *DO*, FORGETTING THOSE THINGS WHICH ARE BEHIND, and reaching forth unto those things which are before, I press toward the mark for the prize of the high calling of God in Christ Jesus.

Philippians 3:13

Even though this book is teaching you to remember, there are some things you must forget. You must forget some of your failures and shrug off discouragement. You must forget about

76

your successes so that they don't give you a false sense of achievement.

Focusing on your past victories can lull you into inactivity and make you complacent. This is why Paul decided to forget the things that were behind him and reach for the things before him.

Chapter 8

People You Must Not Forget

Remove not the ancient landmark, which thy fathers have set.

Proverbs 22:28

As you go through life you will meet some people who mark the turning points of your life. These people are landmarks in your journey to God. You must believe that they did not walk into your life accidentally. They came into your life because God sent them.

Do You Meet People by Accident?

The book of Daniel starts by saying that God delivered Jehoiakim into the hand of Nebuchadnezzar. Meanwhile the secular newspapers may have read, "Jehoiakim was defeated in a battle with Nebuchadnezzar."

But from the view point of Heaven, God had handed over Jehoiakim to Nebuchadnezzar!

In the third year of the reign of Jehoiakim king of Judah came Nebuchadnezzar king of Babylon unto Jerusalem, and besieged it.

And the Lord gave Jehoiakim king of Judah into his hand...

Daniel 1:1-2

God brought Nebuchadnezzar into the picture and displaced Jehoiakim. This was the hand of God. You must believe in the sovereignty of God and that He sends people of His choice into your life. You must welcome and receive whomever God sends into your life.

Instead of fighting the people that God sends to us, we must remember them and honour them. This is the teaching of the Bible. You can see from the Scripture below that many people fight those who are sent to them.

> **... he sent his servants to the husbandmen, that they might receive the fruits of it.**
>
> **And the husbandmen took his servants, and beat one, and killed another, and stoned another.**
>
> **Again, he sent other servants more than the first: and they did unto them likewise.**
>
> Matthew 21:34-36

God is warning us to recognize His messengers.

I try to recognize those who have been sent to me! Do not just relate with people in the natural. Interpret their entrance as a supernatural event. That way, you will benefit from many of the people that God divinely sends to your life.

Ten People You Must Never Forget

1. *Your Soul Winner:* **The person who led you to Christ**

> **For though ye have ten thousand instructors in Christ, yet have ye not many fathers: for in Christ Jesus I HAVE BEGOTTEN YOU through the gospel.**
>
> 1 Corinthians 4:15

Definitely the one who brought you to the Lord will be the most special person in your life. Your greatest treasure is your salvation. The person who helps you to know the Lord is indeed someone never to be forgotten.

Because I came to the Lord through a ministry called Scripture Union, the Lord asked me to remember them and support them. I cannot forget those who sacrificed that I may know the Lord today.

It is presumptuous to assume that salvation was your right. It is through the toil and effort of dedicated Christians that anyone ever hears the Gospel!

2. *Your First Teacher:* **The person who taught you the fundamentals of Christianity**

   ... you have need again for someone to teach you THE ELEMENTARY PRINCIPLES of the oracles of God...
   Hebrews 5:12, NASB

Anyone who comes to Christ will have to be taught elementary principles. The way you are taught the elementary principles of Christ permanently determines your spiritual make-up. Some people start their Christian race with much fasting and prayer. Others are given a strong foundation in the Scriptures.

All these determine how a person will turn out in the Lord. Unfortunately, many of today's charismatic Christians do not have a good foundation in the Lord.

Sadly, many of those who taught them the elementary principles of Christ did not do a thorough job.

I was blessed to have someone who taught me how to have my quiet time. She taught me the basic principles of Christ. She grounded me in the Scripture and made me know that the Bible can be used to answer every practical question of this life. I learnt how to apply the Bible to my everyday life. I cannot forget her; she was my first teacher and she will always be precious in my memory.

3. *Your Inspirer:* **The person who influenced you to go into ministry**

   ... And Eli perceived that the Lord had called the child. Therefore, Eli said unto Samuel, Go, lie down: and it shall be, if he call thee, that thou shalt say, Speak, Lord; for thy servant heareth. So Samuel went and lay down in his place.

And the Lord came, and stood, and called as at other times, Samuel, Samuel. Then Samuel answered, Speak; for thy servant heareth.

1 Samuel 3:8-10

Eli encouraged Samuel to respond to the call of God. Eli was Samuel's trainer and inspirer in the Ministry. If Eli were not there, Samuel would not have been in the Ministry. Samuel would not have known what the call of God was. Look into your life and you will discover who inspired you into Ministry.

Most people in this world would discourage you from being in the Ministry. Many Christians, including ministers, discourage people from being in full-time ministry. But there are some precious few who would encourage you to obey the call of God. These are special people and you must never forget them.

4. *Your Example:* **The person who taught you how to preach**

There are people who come into your life and show you some of the most valuable skills of life. One of the most important skills you will need for your ministry is the ability to preach.

How many people in this world can ever teach you how to preach? There are many Biology, Chemistry and Physics teachers, but how many can teach you how to preach?

If you have been exposed to someone who will show you how to preach, then you have met one of life's rare treasures!

5. *Your Life Teacher:* **The person who taught you about life**

... be thou AN EXAMPLE of the believers, IN WORD, IN CONVERSATION, IN CHARITY, IN SPIRIT, IN FAITH, IN PURITY.

1 Timothy 4:12

Usually, there is someone who teaches you a lot about life. As you can see in the Scripture above, Paul was an example in word and in many other things. Many of us do not have good examples of marriage and home life.

Often you will learn much about life through example setters that God will send to you. God knew that your home would not be able to train you in everything. He has raised up others to fill the gaps in your upbringing. You must learn from these people as well.

6. *Your Trainer:* The person who trained you in ministry

And the things that you have heard from me among many witnesses, commit these to faithful men who will be able to teach others also.

2 Timothy 2:2, NKJV

My first good sermons were the ones that I copied from Kenneth Hagin. There are people through whom you become anointed and seasoned for the work of God. There are also people who will teach you how to pray, how to fast and how to wait on the Lord. Their guidance is invaluable and makes all the difference.

God blessed me with various anointed men through whom I have learnt about ministry. God blessed me and anointed me one day in July 1988 through the person I see as my trainer in the ministry. I loved to listen to him and hear all he had to say about ministry.

I loved to read his books and glean everything I could from them. All that I knew of real ministry I learnt from him. Surely, he was a special trainer sent from God for my life!

I was in a minibus in Nairobi, Kenya when I heard the news that my trainer had died. I was heartbroken and I wept in the bus as we drove to the hotel. I felt as though somebody I had lived with had passed away.

Can there be anybody more precious than the one through whom you gained access to the highest calling ever offered to men? Can you ever forget such a person? Indeed, if the ministry is precious to you, the one who trained you will be a very special person!

7. *Your Launcher:* **The person who gave you an opportunity in ministry**

But BARNABAS TOOK HIM, AND BROUGHT HIM to the apostles, and declared unto them how he had seen the Lord in the way, and that he had spoken to him, and how he had preached boldly at Damascus in the name of Jesus.

Acts 9:27

In December of 1991, my pastor ordained me into the ministry. He laid hands on me and ushered me into the ministry in front of a large congregation in London. After that, he gave me an opportunity to preach in his church. I am always grateful to him for the great honour that was bestowed on me.

You cannot ordain yourself. It is a privilege for a senior in ministry to acknowledge you publicly and recommend you to the congregation. Such people must never be forgotten. Many years have gone by but I have not forgotten how and through whom God launched me into ministry.

8. *Your Father:* **The person who loved you and had faith in you**

Paul was a father to Timothy. Many ministers are simply not fathers. Elijah was a father in the ministry and he left behind a son, Elisha. Elisha had no patience for covetous servants who were not as keen on the anointing as he was. When the opportunity came, Elisha cursed Gehazi and that was the last time we heard of him. Sadly, many great ministers leave no one behind to take after them.

But I hope...to send Timothy to you shortly...But you know of his proven worth, that he served with me in the furtherance of the gospel like a child serving his father.

Philippians 2:19, 22, NASB

A father is someone who has faith in you and loves you. Unfortunately, many ministers are insecure and unable to play the role of a father. I have encountered many great ministers who seem intimidated by my ministry. I rarely felt love or faith coming from these people. Mostly, I sensed suspicion and wariness from people who should have been fathers.

I pray that when it is my turn God will make me a loving father to someone.

9. *Your Forerunner:* The person who goes ahead and fights for you

These are people whose lives are examples for you to learn from. They experience many things right before your eyes and God expects you to watch closely and learn. God has allowed me to see and learn from many wonderful apostles ahead of me. They have fought battles for the entire church and I simply enjoy the benefits of their unfortunate experiences.

Solomon entered into the victories that his father had won. David's whole life was spent fighting one battle after another. By the time David died, there were few enemies for Solomon to conquer. Solomon spent his time building, not fighting. He even used his armies for construction instead of war. Solomon may have seemed to accomplish more, but it was because David had paved the way for him!

Another example of a forerunner is Moses. Moses endured the criticism and hardness of heart of the nation of Israel. He did not have a single day of peace as he led millions of grumbling Israelites. He had to quell one rebellion after another, while at the same time, writing their laws.

By the time Joshua came on the scene, all the grumbling, criticizing people were dead. The entire nation had learnt the lesson of what happens to a discontented, disobedient and unbelieving people. They now knew that their lives depended on having faith and obeying their leader.

Joshua reaped the benefits of Moses' suffering. He enjoyed a ministry with loyal people who would eliminate anyone who dared to grumble.

Whosoever he be that doth rebel against thy commandment, and will not hearken unto thy words in all that thou commandest him, HE SHALL BE PUT TO DEATH: only be strong and of a good courage.

Joshua 1:18

They promised Joshua that they would kill anyone who rebelled against him. Can you see what a different and positive attitude Joshua enjoyed? Moses suffered criticism for years so that Joshua could have an easier ministry. Can you imagine how much more Moses would have achieved if he had had such committed people?

10. *Your Sponsor:* **The person who helped you financially**

Now ye Philippians know also, that...no church communicated with me as concerning giving and receiving, but ye only. For even in Thessalonica ye sent once and again unto my necessity.

Philippians 4:15-16

God used certain people to finance me in the ministry. My big sister supported me in the ministry when I first began. Through her monthly support, I was able to launch out into full-time ministry in 1991. Without her support, I would not be where I am today. I am always grateful and I always remember her privately and publicly.

My own mother has supported me in the ministry. Through her financial support, I was able to live in Ghana and continue in the ministry. This has been God's way of providing for me. How can I forget these people? It would be a sin before the Lord. No matter how the Lord lifts me up and blesses me financially, I must remember those who sponsored me from the very beginning.

Chapter 9

Five Memorials That Fight Against Forgetfulness

G od in His wisdom instituted memorials to help us remember important things that must never be forgotten. In this section, I want to share about the wisdom of memorials that help us to remember.

1. Memorial Feasts

> **Three times a year you shall celebrate a feast to Me.**
> **Exodus 23:14, NASB**

God ordained three main feasts for Israel. These feasts commemorated various significant events in the life of the nation Israel. They were to serve as reminders of significant things that the Lord taught them in their walk with Him.

I am presenting an outline of these three feasts below. These seven different events are grouped into three feast times. The Feast of Passover took place in the first month; the Feast of Pentecost took place in the third month, whilst the Feast of Tabernacles was held in the seventh month of the year.

What You Should Know about the Feast of Passover

For I will go through the land of Egypt on that night, and will strike down all the firstborn in the land of Egypt, both man and beast; and against all the gods of Egypt I will execute judgments - I am the LORD.

> **Now this day will be a memorial to you, and you shall celebrate it as a feast to the LORD; throughout your generations you are to celebrate it as a permanent ordinance.**
> **Exodus 12:12, 14, NASB**

1. The purpose of this feast was to remind the children of Israel of their deliverance from the bondage of Egypt; the passing over of the firstborn.

   He wanted them to always remember what He had done for them so that they would serve Him and trust Him for the future.

2. This feast of Passover was also called the Days of Unleavened Bread. It was ordained by God. "Now the LORD said to Moses and Aaron in the land of Egypt, "This month shall be the beginning of months for you; it is to be the first month of the year to you" (Exodus 12:1-2, NASB).

3. The feast of Passover commenced on the fourteenth day of the first month at even. "In the first month, on the fourteenth day of the month at evening, you shall eat unleavened bread, until the twenty-first day of the month at evening. Seven days there shall be no leaven found in your houses; for whoever eats what is leavened, that person shall be cut off from the congregation of Israel, whether he is an alien or a native of the land" (Exodus 12:18-19, NASB).

4. The feast of Passover lasted seven days during which unleavened bread was eaten. "Seven days you shall eat unleavened bread..." (Exodus 12:15, NASB).

What You Should Know about the Feast of Pentecost

Also you shall observe the Feast of the Harvest of the first fruits of your labors from what you sow in the field...

Exodus 23:16, NASB

1. The purpose of this festival was to celebrate their first fruits. Every first fruit is a blessing from the Lord. The first fruit belongs to God. God instituted this feast to remind the children of Israel of how He provides the blessing of the first fruit.

It is a blessing to have a child. The very first child is the most difficult to have. It is therefore given to the Lord as a special offering. The first part of the harvest is also a special offering to the Lord. It is the tithe and God owns it (Leviticus 27:30).

2. This feast was also called the Day of Pentecost, the Feast of Weeks and the Day of the First Fruits.

3. The Feast of Pentecost was held on the fiftieth day after offering the first sheaf of barley harvest. "You shall also count for yourselves from the day after the Sabbath, from the day when you brought in the sheaf of the wave offering; there shall be seven complete Sabbaths. You shall count fifty days to the day after the seventh Sabbath; then you shall present a new grain offering to the LORD" (Leviticus 23:15-16, NASB).

4. The Feast of Pentecost was to be perpetually observed. "On this same day you shall make a proclamation as well; you are to have a holy convocation. You shall do no laborious work. It is to be a perpetual statute in all your dwelling places throughout your generations" (Leviticus 23:21, NASB).

5. The Feast of Pentecost was to be attended by all. "Three times a year all your males shall appear before the Lord GOD" (Exodus 23:17, NASB).

6. The Feast of Pentecost was a time of holy rejoicing. "And you shall rejoice before the LORD your God..." (Deuteronomy 16:11, NASB).

What You Should Know about the Feast of Tabernacles

... that your generations may know that I made the children of Israel to dwell in booths, when I brought them out of the land of Egypt: I am the LORD your God.

Leviticus 23:43

1. The purpose of the feast was to commemorate the sojourn of Israel in the desert. Once again God wanted the children of Israel not to forget the experience and lessons of the desert.

2. During this feast, they would go into tabernacles and remember what it was like to live in the desert. Imagine moving out of your house every year to go and live in a tent for a week.

   What was the essence of this? God wanted the Israelites to remember the experiences of the desert. He wanted them to remember all the lessons of those forty years. Do not black out and delete your wilderness days. Every painful experience you have had is intended to be remembered. Remember your *siniazos*. The Greek word *siniazo* means to "shake in a seive" and to "cause inward agitation and to try one's faith to the verge of overthrow".

3. This feast of tabernacles commenced with a day of blowing of trumpets and was held on the first day of the seventh month. This was a memorial of blowing trumpets, a holy convocation and rest. Sacrifices were made at this festival.

4. During the Feast of Tabernacles people dwelt in tents. "You shall live in booths for seven days; all the native-born in Israel shall live in booths" (Leviticus 23:42, NASB).

5. The Feast of Tabernacles was also called the Feast of Booths. "Speak to the sons of Israel, saying, "On the fifteenth of this seventh month is the Feast of Booths for seven days to the LORD" (Leviticus 23:34, NASB).

6. The Feast of Tabernacles was held after harvest. "You shall celebrate the Feast of Booths seven days after you have gathered in from your threshing floor and your wine vat" (Deuteronomy 16:13, NASB).

7. The Feast of Tabernacles began on the fifteenth day of the seventh month. "On the fifteenth of this seventh month..." (Leviticus 23:34, NASB).

8. The Feast of Tabernacles lasted seven days. "...the Feast of Booths for seven days to the LORD" (Leviticus 23:34, NASB).

9. The Feast of Tabernacles required all males to attend. "Three times a year all your males shall appear before the Lord GOD" (Exodus 23:17, NASB).

10. The Feast of Tabernacles were to be days off regular work. "On the first day is a holy convocation; you shall do no laborious work of any kind. On exactly the fifteenth day of the seventh month, when you have gathered in the crops of the land, you shall celebrate the feast of the LORD for seven days, with a rest on the first day and a rest on the eighth day" (Leviticus 23:35,39, NASB).

11. The Feast of Tabernacles was to be perpetually observed. "On this same day you shall make a proclamation as well; you are to have a holy convocation. You shall do no laborious work. It is to be a perpetual statute in all your dwelling places throughout your generations" (Leviticus 23:21, NASB).

12. The Feast of Tabernacles was a time of holy rejoicing. "And you shall rejoice before the LORD your God..." (Deuteronomy 16:11, NASB).

2. Memorial Ceremonies

Now Elisabeth's full time came that she should be delivered; and she brought forth a son.

And her neighbours and her cousins heard how the Lord had shewed great mercy upon her; and they rejoiced with her.

And it came to pass, that on the eighth day they came to circumcise the child; and they called him Zacharias, after the name of his father.

Luke 1:57-59

John the Baptist was named and dedicated a few days after his birth. His entrance into this world was marked by a little home ceremony. This ceremony was recorded in the Bible and for all time reminds us of the supernatural birth of John.

God also instituted ceremonies so that we would not forget important covenants that we have made. Weddings and baby dedications are common ceremonies we know about. It is possible to get married without any ceremony whatsoever. A declaration by a pastor will initiate a marriage between two people if they believe in the pastor's pronouncement.

Most people however do not enter this covenant lightly or without ceremony. They mark the event with much expense on decorations, dresses, food and jollity. Because the marital covenant is marked with such ceremony, it is not easy to break or to disengage from. Such is the power of ceremonial memorials. These ceremonies go a long way to remind us of important covenants we make.

3. Memorials and Monuments

And Joshua said unto them, Pass over before the ark of the Lord your God into the midst of Jordan, and take ye up every man of you a stone upon his shoulder, according unto the number of the tribes of the children of Israel:

That this may be A SIGN among you, that when your children ask their fathers in time to come, saying, What mean ye by these stones?

Then ye shall answer them, THAT THE WATERS OF JORDAN WERE CUT OFF BEFORE THE ARK of the covenant of the Lord; when it passed over Jordan, the waters of Jordan were cut off: and these stones shall be for a memorial unto the children of Israel for ever.

Joshua 4:5-7

There are times that monuments need to be set up to keep our memories alive. Sometimes things have to be named after someone in order to remember the person's contribution. London is a city of monuments and memories, whereas many other cities have no monuments and remember no one.

I named one of the chapels in our church "Adelaide Chapel" in order to remember my wife's contribution to my life and ministry. It is an important memorial for the future. As the number of people working in the ministry increases, the contribution of faithful people is often forgotten.

One day, I went to a church in which the pastor's wife had died. Several things were named after his former wife. There was no way you could spend a day in the church without remembering her contribution. There was a new wife but the first wife was remembered!

4. Memorial Rituals

And when he had given thanks, he brake it, and said, Take, eat: this is my body, which is broken for you: this do IN REMEMBRANCE of me.

After the same manner also he took the cup, when he had supped, saying, This cup is the new testament in my blood: this do ye, as oft as ye drink it, IN REMEMBRANCE of me.

For as often as ye eat this bread, and drink this cup, ye do shew the Lord's death till he come.

1 Corinthians 11:24-26

Our Lord Jesus instituted the ritual of communion to remind us of His death. One day, the deacons of a church slipped a note on the pulpit of the pastor of a huge church. The note had a simple message and it said, "Pastor, we would see Jesus." They actually quoted from a passage in John 12:21: "The same came therefore to Philip, which was of Bethsaida of Galilee, and desired him, saying, SIR, WE WOULD SEE JESUS."

The pastor was stunned. He struggled through his sermon that morning and slipped into his study. He could not believe the message he had received from the deacons. But he understood what it meant!

The pastor said later, "When I saw the note, I knew immediately what it meant. I had drifted from preaching about Christ to giving good advice for life. My sermons were just tips to solve the felt needs of the people. I knew I had shifted from teaching about Jesus Christ. I had left true Scripture and had become a teacher of success, positive thinking and self-empowerment."

Just as those Greeks were not interested in seeing Philip but wanted to see Jesus Himself, the people who come to our churches want to see Jesus. People who come to our churches need Jesus! Sadly, we ministers often sideline Christ Jesus. But Jesus must be the centre and focus of all that we do.

This is why the Lord instituted the ritual of the Lord's Supper. It is easy to drift from the main thing. But the main thing will always be the main thing!

Satan loves to push Christians onto roads that are close and parallel to the real road. He urges us on into good things that are not God's will. Through demonic guidance, there is a lot of Christian activity but much of God's purpose is set aside.

5. Supernatural Memorials

Paul's Supernatural Reminder

As you serve the Lord and obey His Word, He will lift you up. But it is easy to forget that you are a nonentity who is being blessed by Almighty God. Our fleshly nature tends to pride as quickly as a stone drops from a height. God in His mercy must send messengers of Satan to buffet us so that we will not be lifted up in pride.

The messengers of Satan are supernatural reminders that constantly remind us of our mortality and nothingness. Perhaps, if it were not for some of these supernatural reminders we would shoot off on a tangent and claim to be super successful heroes who know it all.

And lest I should be exalted above measure through the abundance of the revelations, there was given to me

93

a thorn in the flesh, the messenger of Satan to buffet me, lest I should be exalted above measure.

2 Corinthians 12:7

I thank God for the things that He has sent to buffet me. One day, the Lord said to me that He was sorry that He had had to allow certain things to happen in my life. He told me that He had blessed me with much more in the ministry than many others would ever dream of.

The Holy Spirit showed me that the potential pride-filling effect of these blessings was very dangerous. He had therefore given me messengers of Satan who would box me into a pitiful state where I would find myself falling to my knees in helplessness. He told me that these messengers of Satan were necessary to protect me from pride and other spiritual evils.

Sometimes when I am buffeted, I am brought so low that I feel worse than the lowest wretch.

I ask myself, "How can the weakest person be the pastor of the church? How can someone whose prayers are not answered lead a congregation? How can someone who is depressed help anyone else?"

At these times, I see nothing victorious or successful about my ministry. Through the buffeting messages my knees are brought to the ground and tears fall out of my eyes.

God told me to embrace (and not fight) these distressing things, which are reproaches and infirmities in my life. Indeed, I have come to discover that when I take pleasure in these infirmities, the power of Christ rests on me.

... Most gladly, therefore, I will rather boast about my weaknesses, so that the power of Christ may dwell in me.

2 Corinthians 12:9, NASB

Nebuchadnezzar's Supernatural Reminder

Nebuchadnezzar had a mental illness, which reminded him that God was in charge of this world and not him! Nebuchadnezzar needed this supernatural reminder to bring him down to size. He was told:

... O king, and this is the decree of the Most High, which has come upon my lord the king: that YOU BE DRIVEN AWAY FROM MANKIND and your dwelling place be with the beasts of the field, and you be given grass to eat like cattle and be drenched with the dew of heaven; and seven periods of time will pass over you, UNTIL YOU RECOGNIZE THAT THE MOST HIGH IS RULER over the realm of mankind and bestows it on whomever He wishes.

Daniel 4:24-25, NASB

After this supernatural reminder, Nebuchadnezzar was transformed into a humble king. He lived and reigned humbly after God supernaturally reminded him of whom he really was.

Belshazzar's Supernatural Reminder

Belshazzar, the son of Nebuchadnezzar equally needed a supernatural reminder to bring him down to size. Unfortunately, his reminder came on the day of his death. God expected him to have learnt from his father's life, especially his father's mental illness.

And thou his son, O Belshazzar, hast not humbled thine heart, though thou knewest all this; then was the part of the hand sent from him; and this writing was written.

Daniel 5:22, 24

Sometimes, something that happens to someone just ahead of you is a supernatural reminder of the way to go and the things to avoid. May your eyes be opened to understand the supernatural reminders that are placed before you!

The Conclusion

It is my prayer, O my son that this treatise which I have endeavoured to share with you on the subject of remembrance, will be embedded in your heart.

To the making of many books, there is indeed no end!

I therefore must come to a conclusion here. I pray that God will bless you with lasting loyalty so that one day, you will hear those blessed words, "Well done, good and faithful servant."